SAM NORKIN

SAM NORKIN

DRAWINGS • STORIES

*for Wendy
from
the Cornyetzs*

THEATER OPERA BALLET MOVIES

HEINEMANN
PORTSMOUTH, NH

HEINEMANN
A division of Reed Elsevier Inc.
361 Hanover Street
Portsmouth, NH 03801-3912

Offices and agents throughout the world

© 1994 by Sam Norkin.

Editor:
Lisa A. Barnett

Production:
Renee M. Pinard

Interior:
Sam Norkin
Jenny Jensen Greenleaf

Cover: Sam Norkin

Library of Congress Cataloging-in-Publication Data

Norkin, Sam.
  Sam Norkin : drawings, stories.
      p.   cm.
  Includes index.
  ISBN 0-435-08642-1
  1. Norkin, Sam.   2. Entertainers—United States—Caricatures and cartoons.   3. American wit and humor, Pictorial.   4. Entertainers—United States—Anecdotes.   I. Title.   II. Title: Drawings, stories.
  NC1429.N67A4   1994
  741.5'973—dc20   94-29122
                                                                  CIP

Front cover subjects, upper panel, top row, l. to r.: Bette Davis (for Norkin exhibit ad); Marlon Brando (*A Streetcar Named Desire*); Joan Sutherland (concert appearance); Tallulah Bankhead (*Midgie Purvis*). **Bottom row, l. to r.:** James Earl Jones (*Fences*); Suzanne Farrell (*Afternoon of a Faun*); Colleen Dewhurst (*A Moon for the Misbegotten*). **Lower panel, top row, l. to r.:** Basil Rathbone (as Sherlock Holmes, film); Zero Mostel (*A Funny Thing Happened on the Way to the Forum*); Laurence Olivier (*The Betsy*, film). **Bottom row, l. to r.:** Katherine Hepburn (*A Matter of Gravity*); Ethel Merman (*Annie Get Your Gun*); Jonathan Pryce (*Miss Saigon*).

Back cover subjects, top row, l. to r.: Helen Hayes (*The Show-off*); Mikhail Baryshnikov (*The Prodigal Son*); Lou Jacobi (*Don't Drink the Water*). **Center row, l. to r.:** Barbra Streisand (TV special); Lena Horne (*The Lady and Her Music*); Eugene Ormandy (Conductor, Philadelphia Orchestra). **Bottom row, l. to r.:** Dustin Hoffman (*The Merchant of Venice*); Richard Kiley (*Man of La Mancha*); Tyne Daly (*Gypsy*).

Printed in the United States of America on acid-free paper
99 98 97 96 95 94   1 2 3 4 5 6 7 8 9

DEDICATION

To Francie, my wife, partner, and playgoing companion. She is a
no-nonsense critic, whereas I sometimes equivocate. When uncertain
about matters of audience reaction, I can depend on Francie for
a straightforward opinion. Francie's fun-loving side enables her
to speak while laughing. It is a relaxing thing to know your
humor is always appreciated.

PROLOGUE

Thinking back over the twenty-odd seasons I've been studying Sam's Sunday drawings preparatory to a week's playgoing, I realize that Norkin's sense of drama has shown a disturbing tendency to win out over the playwright's. Time and again, the Monday, Tuesday, or Thursday evening hasn't lived up to the promise of Sunday morning. In fact, there have been occasions when I'd have much preferred the mental image of Sam's sketch to remain unspoiled by the show, just as I'd rather look at his famous hippo than wallow through most circus numbers.

There is an enviable mastery at work here, and ranging through the Norkin catalogue one experiences not just the tingle of remembered pleasures in the theater but, along with them, sudden smiles and, now and then, reawakened terrors. His is an astonishing and valuable art.

DOUGLAS WATT
Drama Critic Emeritus
New York Daily News

In 1961, after I learned there was such a thing as legitimate theater, I was happy to discover that my hometown of Arlington, Massachusetts, was only twelve miles away from three legitimate playhouses. Boston's Shubert and Colonial were the places to see the big musicals, and the Wilbur hosted the plays and comedies.

The first pre-Broadway tryout I ever saw was *I Can Get It for You Wholesale*, which I loved—especially because it allowed me to be the first on my block to discover Barbra Streisand. Twenty-two months later, I was hungering for her *Funny Girl*.

In between, I lusted for *Mr. President*, *Beyond the Fringe*, *Never Too Late*, *110 in the Shade*, and *The Girl Who Came to Supper*. After *Funny Girl* fled to Philadelphia, there was something called *Never Live over a Pretzel Factory* sandwiched among Richard Burton in *Hamlet*, Sammy Davis in *Golden Boy*, and Robert Preston in *Ben Franklin in*

Paris. And how I looked forward to Carol Burnett in *A Girl to Remember*, even when its name was changed to *The Idol of Millions* and then, again, to *Fade Out—Fade In*.

The pattern was always the same. Every Sunday morning I'd tear open the *Boston Globe* to find the theater section, which each week carried some valuable information for this fast-budding showfreak. First came the announcement of what new show was coming to town. Next the ad with the logo.

And then came the Sam Norkin drawing.

From the ad, I would have already learned that Oliver Smith, Robert Randolph, or William and Jean Eckart would be doing the sets. That Miles White, Freddy Wittop, or Florence Klotz would design the costumes. But the first hint of what they'd actually look like came from Sam Norkin.

Through Sam I discovered that *The Odd Couple* had a poker-playing scene. That *High Spirits* featured a séance. That Liza Minnelli would wear a tam-o'-shanter in *Flora, the Red Menace*. And though *The Apple Tree* dropped the ornate, elaborate set from its Garden of Eden sequence just days before its Boston bow, I got a hint of what it was like—through a Sam Norkin drawing, of course.

The images stay with me: Mary Martin hat-'n'-caning her way

through *Jennie*. Ruth Gordon with one arm akimbo, ready to tell about all *The Loves of Cass McGuire*. Alfred Drake on his knees and pleading for justice in *Lorenzo*. For that matter, the first time I ever saw any kind of picture of Vivien Leigh was Sam's drawing for *Tovarich*. That was before I even knew she'd been in a movie called *Gone With the Wind*. Don't forget, those were the days when you could see it only once every seven years—and I'd missed the last go-around.

No problem. These days, I can see *Gone With the Wind* any time I want. But I'm much more grateful that I was around for the era when shows came to Boston—and that I had Sam Norkin to give me a preview of all those coming attractions.

—PETER FILICHIA
New Jersey critic, *Newark Star Ledger*
Columnist, *TheaterWeek*
Author, *Let's Put On A Musical*
President, Drama Desk

Some years ago I was visiting Alan Schneider, that fine director, and his lovely wife, Jean, at their condo in East Hampton.

We were a group of theater people sitting around in his cozy living room, surrounded by stage memorabilia, and naturally we gravitated to the telling of theater stories. I soaked them up with great pleasure and was then reminded by my wife, Francie, to offer my Molnár story. She was referring to my all-time favorite, as told to me by that unsurpassed yarn spinner, playwright Ferenc Molnár. I knew, when I heard it many years earlier, that it would never be topped and I have attempted to do him justice in its retelling ever since. It was followed by a few more tales.

As we were leaving, Schneider said I was a fine raconteur and that my theater stories were some of the best he had ever heard, which made me quite light-headed for the drive home.

But it wasn't until his tragic death and the publication of his autobiography that I realized how significant his remark was. On a number of occasions in his book he referred to spending entire evenings with truly eminent theater people "telling theater stories."

Willy-nilly, I have been witness to material for such stories throughout my experience and have used many in my lecture-demonstrations on the art of caricature, given in colleges, museums, and clubs, on cruises, and at corporate events.

Over three thousand of my theater drawings, dating from the forties, have appeared in newspapers, such as the *Philadelphia Inquirer*, *Washington Post*, *Boston Globe*, and *Toronto Star*, across the continent; and in New York City, for over twenty-five years, every week in the *Daily News* and in the *Herald Tribune* earlier. It was that great PR man Dick Maney who arranged for newspapers in the theatrical tryout cities to print my drawings of shows sketched mainly at dress rehearsals in New York. As a result, I have attended more rehearsals than anyone else in the field.

From the beginning, I wrote my own captions because I was working from advance materials. Without my information, Arthur Folwell, my editor at the *Herald Tribune*, would tend to be inaccurate. Shortly after I came to the *Daily News*, John Chapman, my new boss, gave orders to the staff to use my captions verbatim. Eventually my intensive involvement with the performing arts made me useful to my editors as an extra critic and writer. I also initiated art reviews in the *Daily News* after a two-year stint in the Carnegie Hall House Program. My drawings have been appearing in *American Theater* magazine, *Stages*, *TheaterWeek*, and *Back Stage*.

I am as involved as ever in theatrical affairs. As past president of the Drama Desk, I have been active on the board of directors. For many years, I was also a nominator on its awards committee. I see and sketch all the worthwhile Broadway and off-Broadway shows.

Most important, I have finally crystalized the material I have been gathering for years. There's a story or pertinent nugget of information conjured up by almost every one of my drawings as I view them again.

Some readers may be interested in the author as a person. In the course of presenting my material, I have produced a kind of professional autobiography. The stories behind the drawings reveal my views, values, and background. In my audience there are those to whom the names will spark recognition. Others will find the theater milieu itself of interest. After reading my book, for example, you will never be surprised to hear that a scheduled rehearsal rarely starts on time. It sometimes fails to happen at all.

You will also discover that a change in cast "for artistic differences" means an actor or director has been fired. Or that a play "postponed for rewrites" usually bombed in tryouts and is gone forever.

SAM NORKIN

THE PIANO LESSON

During the 1989–90 season, August Wilson's latest play on the Black Experience, *The Piano Lesson*, opened on Broadway after touring the United States for over two years, winning the Pulitzer prize and generally high praise from the critics. Earlier plays in the series, *Ma Rainey's Black Bottom*, *Fences*, and *Joe Turner's Come and Gone*, had established the playwright's purpose and reputation. With the success of his latest play, it surprised many when so respected an authority as Robert Brustein wrote that Wilson ought to be addressing issues other than the Black Experience.

Inevitably this had to be interpreted as the sour grapes of a man who left the Yale Repertory before director Lloyd Richards took over and produced the successful series there.

The scene from *The Piano Lesson* sketched here was observed with pleasure at the unusual staging of it. The piano in question is a family heirloom bearing symbolic biographical carvings and its proposed sale is the subject of controversy. At one point, to the glee of those present, a relative plays it. Charles S. Dutton, in the lead, gets into the spirit of the moment and is carried away in dance—not as seen here, facing front for identification—but with his back to the audience! I commented to him sometime later how impressed I was with director Richards's subtle method. By having Dutton's back to the audience he avoided making it a "number" in "a play with music." Dutton quickly disabused me of my keen perception. The extrovert performer confided to me that he was "too bashful" to face front while dancing, despite Richards's urging him to do so!

The Piano Lesson. L. to r.: Lou Myers, S. Epatha Merkerson, Rocky Carrol, Charles S. Dutton, Carl Gordon. *Stages* 1990.

Winner of the Pulitzer Prize. Charles Gordone's *No Place to Be Somebody.* L. to r.: Nathan George, Marge Eliot, Ronnie Thompson, Susan Pearson, Ron O'Neal, and Walter Jones. *New York Daily News* 1969.

When I am privileged to be the only outsider at a rehearsal, the director may relate to me in the following ways: Ignore me, if he thinks he has a hit; give me succinct information in a professional manner; buy me a pastrami sandwich and stage any scene I desire if he suspects he is stuck with a bomb; put on an ego show strictly for my benefit.

In the several times I witnessed the late Otto Preminger in action, it was his performance I found infinitely more entertaining than the play he was shaping.

Full Circle, a play originally in German by Erich Maria Remarque, was adapted by Peter Stone, who was present along with Remarque's widow, Paulette Goddard. The Fall of Berlin from the Nazis to the Soviets was the theme.

At one point, Preminger lost patience with a bit player, stood up from his seat in the first row, and in his German accent shouted, "Ve cut your twenty lines down to *vun* line and now you are blowing dat *vun* line! You vill drive me up ze vall und I'll chump off!"

To Ms. Goddard, producer of the play, tiptoeing in from the street, across the corner of the stage, to the seats, with coffee for all, he bellowed, "Have ve no security at ze stage door?!! Must ve have all zese interruptions?"

When Peter Stone approached him during a scene and whispered in his ear, he rose and roared, "Vot can ve expect ven ze author himself interrupts his own play?"

Preminger, in his time, visited his Prussian tyranny on many of the actors he directed. It is said that in one backstage insurrection, all cast members signed a petition to have him removed. One actor refused. When asked why, he answered, "My parents are still in Germany."

Otto Preminger, left, directing *Full Circle*. Josef Sommer, Leonard Nimoy, Bibi Andersson.
New York Daily News 1973.

ARTHUR KOPIT

The drawing seen here of Arthur Kopit's play *Wings*, depicting Constance Cummings as a former illustrious aviatrix now in the throes of a stroke, evoked the most positive response I ever received. I tried to reflect the disorientation, enhanced by lighting effects, as registered onstage of Ms. Cummings in her award-winning performance.

Unlike Tennessee Williams or Arthur Miller, whose plays evoke expected flavors, Arthur Kopit is wildly unpredictable in the diversification of his themes. *Oh Dad, Poor Dad, Momma's Hung You in the Closet and I'm Feelin' So Sad*, another award winner, deals with a son and his domineering mother; *Indians* is about government injustice visited on our native Americans; *The Road to Nirvana* is a 1991 devastation of Hollywood that staged profane figures of speech literally, such as "You want my blood?" "You're making me eat shit," and "She wants my balls."

In 1982 Kopit won a Tony for his book for Best Musical, *Nine*, based on Fellini's *8½*. His collaborator, composer Maury Yeston, joined him again for their version of *The Phantom of the Opera*, well received out of town, but not seemingly ready for a tussle with the long-running Lloyd Webber *Phantom* on Broadway.

Wings. Constance Cummings. *New York Daily News* 1979.

Indians. L. to r.: Manu, Stacy Keach, George Mitchell. *New York Daily News* 1969.

Oh Dad, Poor Dad, Momma's Hung You in the Closet and I'm Feelin' So Sad.
Top: Hermione Gingold. Sandor Szabo. Below: Alix Elias, Sam Waterston.
New York Daily News 1963.

Among my treasured memories of the theater are the fabulous comic dancing team, The Hartmans (Grace and Paul). Their signature act was set in a glittering ballroom, extravagantly draped, flowered, and chandeliered. As a velvety waltz theme set the stage, the suave pair glided into view, all elegance; he, a poised continental, she, a lady of supreme grace. But, can it be? In one turn, his toe caught her hem and opened a gash at the waistline. In a swirl, her grasp disengaged his entire sleeve. And so it continued until nothing was left but his boxer shorts and Paris garters, and her chemise.

They were never better than in the revue *Tickets, Please*, which also included hilarious sketches performed by the pair. My drawing of their "Fire Dance" number, in which she was the elusive flame pursued by an earnest water carrier, appeared in the *New York Herald Tribune*. The producer purchased the drawing for use on window cards and subway posters and presented the Hartmans with the original art.

Some years later, I met Paul at a rehearsal. He took me aside and said he had a sad little story to tell, of special interest to me. He had taken the drawing to a firm that bakes such mementos onto porcelain plates. It was suggested that, because of the vertical shape of the artwork, it would be best if Paul and Grace were placed in larger sizes on two separate round plates. Paul agreed, and by the time the plates were delivered, the Hartmans themselves had separated.

Tickets, Please. Grace and Paul Hartman in the "Fire Dance." *New York Herald Tribune* c. 1950.

From Miracle in the Mountains to Miracle Worker

A proliferation of productions followed the great success of *The Miracle Worker*, William Gibson's moving play about how Annie Sullivan brought communication to the blind and deaf child Helen Keller. Anne Bancroft was Sullivan and Patty Duke became a young star even though she spoke but one word, at the end, as Helen.

I was struck by an ad in *Variety* at the time, seeking American youngsters to play Helen Keller in European productions. The ad assured candidates that language was no problem because the character spoke only that word. Still, I wondered why the producer didn't cast European children along with the rest of the European companies.

Suddenly I remembered why. Europe, it seems, has no tradition of child actors. They rarely appear on stage, and when they do, little is demanded of them. I was taken back to 1946, when I sketched a rehearsal of *Miracle in the Mountains*, a new play by the illustrious Hungarian Ferenc Molnár, escapee from Hitler and author of *The Guardsman*, *The Play's the Thing*, and *Liliom* (the source of *Carousel*) to name a few. In his first play here, he was taking the opportunity to revive a tale involving an illegitimate child who becomes a thorn in the side of his father, the mayor of the town.

I was invited to join the production staff for a lunch break at Roth's Grill. As we sat around the large table, Molnár asked the stage manager if he could count on the kid playing the key role.

"Mr. Molnár, you keep worrying about that and I keep assuring you that the boy has attended the finest acting schools and has Broadway experience in *On Borrowed Time* and *Tomorrow, the World*. I can safely say that at the age of seven, he is a seasoned trouper."

"Well, let me tell you why I worry." And in his rich Hungarian accent, Molnár related the following story:

"Back in the days of Max Reinhardt's Vienna Repertory, he staged a play by Schiller about the Crusades. In the key scene the knight returns after ten years to find a five-year-old boy with his wife. Now, this five-year-old had no lines at all, so one night, when he was down with the measles, a replacement had to be found in a hurry. The stage manager's nephew, familiar with the theater but never on a stage, was pressed into service with the instructions that once in costume, all he had to do was stand still on a spot for a few minutes and the others would do the rest.

"He was put in place, upstage center. The hero entered, asked who the kid was, and the wife confessed her weakness. After all, it's been ten long years.

"With that he began his big speech about loyalty and fidelity in a voice expanding in decibels, suddenly unsheathing a screeching sword and raising it on high as he strode forward.

Ferenc Molnár
1947

"At this point, the kid wets himself and is soon standing in a pool of it. Now I must tell you that the stage is raked, and painted to simulate flagstones. The paint is flat grey, the kind that turns black when wet. So the pool can be seen from the furthest reaches of the balcony. Still worse, the pool turns into a stream because of the slant and is slowly headed downstage to the apron.

"The suspense is now building to an unbearable pitch. Not because of the knight's big speech and menacing saber, but—and I forgot to tell you—in Europe we have a prompter's box in the theaters, such as you have here in the Metropolitan Opera. The audience is now on the edge of its seat, spellbound by what may happen when the stream reaches the prompter. The worst seats in the house, A42–44, are now

the best; they can see the prompter in profile from that corner.

"Suddenly, as the moment of truth approaches, a hand reaches out of the prompter's box, and diverts the stream to the side, sending it sizzling into the footlights.

"Today, years later, they are still laughing about it in Vienna, and that's why I want to know: can we trust this kid?"

The Miracle Worker. Anne Bancroft and Patty Duke. *New York Daily News* 1960.

When you think of Helen Hayes, "First Lady of the American Stage," you are apt to associate her with Queen Victoria in *Victoria Regina* or with Harriet Beecher Stowe in *Harriet*. But her career has been studded with fine comic performances, too, and during the summer of 1947 she was having a great time commuting from her home in Nyack, on the shores of the Hudson, to a comedy by Anita Loos, *Happy Birthday*. She sang and danced every night, receiving the first Tony ever given for Best Actress in a Play.

I was assigned by the *Herald Tribune* to visit Hayes at her home. Needless to say, it was a memorable day for me. I was given a tour of the house, named "Pretty Penny" by husband Charles MacArthur with reference to its cost, shown the theatrical collectibles and the lush garden, introduced to her two poodles and the neighborhood children using her pool, and treated to fine lunch and conversation. I made sketches at every break and was driven back to the city with her in a limo right to the stage door.

The following Sunday, Abner Klipstein, press agent for *Happy Birthday*, was awakened by his wife and informed that Helen Hayes was calling. Abner's first thought as he reached for the phone was that I had somehow offended his star.

Instead he heard a sustained rave about my three personalized sketches in that morning's *Herald Tribune*. One with the poodles, another with the kids, a third with Hayes in a playsuit, clipping flowers.

George Kelly's *The Show-Off*. Helen Hayes and Clayton Corzatte. *New York Daily News* 1968.

Helen Hayes in her Nyack garden.
New York Herald Tribune 1947.

Happy Birthday. L. to r.: Enid Markey, Helen Hayes, Robert Burton, Jack Diamond,
Louis Jean Heydt, Lorraine Miller. *New York Herald Tribune* 1947.

Mrs. McThing. L. to r.: Frank Corsaro, Fred Gwynne, Jules Munshin, Brandon de Wilde, Helen Hayes.
New York Compass 1952.

The Front Page. L. to r.: Charles White, Bernie West, John McGiver, Helen Hayes, Robert Ryan, Kendall March, Bert Convy, Harold J. Kennedy, Dody Goodman, Peggy Cass, Patrick Desmond (in desk).
New York Daily News 1969.

ROMEO AND JULIET
IN STRATFORD, CONNECTICUT

Given the careless approach to simple good speech in our time, it is asking far too much of high school students to embrace, without thorough indoctrination, a true appreciation of Shakespeare. The effort goes on, however, and the American Shakespeare Festival at Stratford, Connecticut had a valiant idea: to polish up by presenting a month of previews to students, and then open in top shape for the regular summer audiences.

I took advantage of one of those student previews to sketch a production of *Romeo and Juliet* in time for the official opening.

All went smoothly until hothead Tybalt stabbed Mercutio as he tried to stop a duel between the feuding families. One of the bit players was sent running for a doctor. In this staging, he exited down a long flight of stairs in the pit before the stage apron and under the audience—and a little too rapidly for safety. He stumbled noisily, unseen but heard all too clearly, ending with a thunderous crash. The young audience exploded with prolonged laughter, and Mercutio's upcoming best lines were about to be smothered by it. William Smithers, playing Mercutio, did not intend to be smothered, so those lines, usually squeezed out with the pain of a dying man, before a hushed audience, were instead shouted: "The wound was not as deep as a well nor as wide as a barn door, but 'twould suffice, and a plague on both your houses."

Unintended laughter continued during the rest of the play, but topping everything was the tragic death scene of the lovers. In a strange piece of staging, Romeo stood astride Juliet's supine body atop her elevated bier, so that when he poisoned himself to join her in death, he had no place to fall but directly upon her, like a blanket. Slowly she came to from her sleeping potion, looked at the audience, and uttered her line, "Where is my Romeo?" Even I had to join the laughter.

Romeo and Juliet. Top: Richard Easton, Inga Swenson. Center: William Smithers, Jack Bittner. Bottom: Morris Carnovsky, Aline MacMahon. *New York Daily News* 1959.

The tryout city for *Do Re Mi*, a hit musical about the jukebox craze, was Philadelphia. Producer David Merrick, who at one point in his career had six hits running on Broadway, led his troupe into town for the premiere. After checking into his hotel, he headed straight for the Shubert Theater to see that all was in order.

He hadn't even arrived at the theater when he spotted trouble a hundred feet away. "Look at that marquee," he groaned to Garson Kanin, the show's author. "It reads 'Do Mi Re'! Where the hell is Bill Doll?" (the show's publicist, in charge of such matters).

"What can I do for you, David?" asked a placid Doll as he sauntered over to the fuming Merrick.

"Read that marquee, that's all!"

Doll looked up, paused, and said, "Well, David, that's why we're out of town!"

Do Re Mi. Phil Silvers, Steve Roland, George Mathews, George Givot, Nancy Walker, and David Burns. *New York Daily News* 1961.

Paradoxically, comedians are apt to be dead serious in rehearsal. Bert Lahr, a celebrated worrier, had no time for humor before he got to work, but when he did he was a riot. Zero Mostel was another story. Always "on," he never missed the chance for a laugh. So when I showed up to sketch him and co-star Eli Wallach in Ionesco's surrealist play *Rhinoceros*, wherein vulnerable members of the population turn into the horned beasts, Mostel greeted me and took me aside to whisper, "Here's twenty dollars. Keep Eli out of the drawing!"

Rhinoceros. Zero Mostel and Eli Wallach. *New York Daily News* 1961.

Painting. Zero Mostel in *Rhinoceros.* 1961.

In December 1946, I dropped in to the press agent's office for some photos to supplement my sketch reference for a drawing of *Beggar's Holiday*, with a score by Duke Ellington. It was based on John Gay's *The Beggar's Opera*, same source as Kurt Weill's *The Threepenny Opera*. There I encountered Zero Mostel, who was playing Peacham and, artist that he was, suggesting logo art for the production. The irrepressible Zero insisted that we sketch each other. Here is his version of me.

THE THREEPENNY OPERA

In 1928, Kurt Weill and Bertolt Brecht's *Die Dreigroschenoper* opened in Berlin, establishing a huge following during a five-year run in pre-Hitler Germany. Many other European productions sprung up well into the thirties. It was tried on Broadway in 1933, but apparently America wasn't quite ready for it. With the Nazi rise to power, Brecht and Weill fled Germany. Hitler destroyed all recordings and other vestiges of the leftist work. A 1931 German movie version and some shellac recordings survived abroad.

Enter Marc Blitzstein, composer of *The Cradle Will Rock*, who freely translated Brecht's text. In 1954 *The Threepenny Opera* opened to enthusiastic reviews and had a respectable run at the Theater de Lys in Greenwich Village. After it closed, every succeeding play at that theater was a disappointment to *New York Times* critic Brooks Atkinson, who closed each review with a plea to "bring back *Threepenny Opera!*" Eventually producers Capalbo and Chase took Atkinson's entreaties seriously and did indeed restore it to the Theater de Lys. It ran some five more years and became an off-Broadway institution. Louis Armstrong recorded the opening number, "Mack the Knife," which made the charts and helped popularize the show.

Now the producers began to flex their muscles and felt the time was right for a national company. Popular former burlesque queen and author Gypsy Rose Lee was cast as Jenny and reinforced by some members of the New York cast, and an extensive tour was booked, starting in Toronto.

There are instances where taste in the continent's heartland differs sharply from what appeals to New York and this was certainly one of them. The reception was dismal in Toronto and the tour was abruptly curtailed. My drawing also played in but one city.

Another version was produced by the New York City Opera for a few performances under Julius Rudel. Joseph Papp presented his own successful production—a bolder, more authentic translation starring Raul Julia—for a limited engagement at Lincoln Center.

Again, national distribution was contemplated in the form of an elaborate color film by Joseph E. Levine. Few people are aware of this project. I sketched it at a screening but the film was withheld as commercially risky. Curt Jurgens was Mack the Knife and Sammy Davis, Jr., the Streetsinger. My drawing never got out of the press kit.

The Threepenny Opera. Joseph Papp Production. L. to r.: C. K. Alexander, Blair Brown, Ellen Greene, Raul Julia, Caroline Kava, Elizabeth Wilson. *New York Daily News* 1976.

In 1989, another film version was made, in Hungary, with Raul Julia again playing Mack the Knife. He and the movie were poorly received and once again, *Threepenny* quickly disappeared.

Enter rock star Sting. His Broadway performance in *3 Penny Opera* was called bland and despite his huge following, the show closed after a short run.

Conclusion: stage *Threepenny Opera* in New York, with spunk. Don't tour it or expect it to succeed as a movie.

Threepenny Opera. For National Tour. Foreground: Gypsy Rose Lee, Scott Merrill.
Closed in first stop: Toronto. *Toronto Star* c. 1959.

3 Penny Opera. Sting, as MacHeath, brandishes cane-sword as Mack the Knife to admiring glances from his brothel friends. *Stages* 1989.

Typifying a trend in recent years, *The Phantom of the Opera* opened in 1987, after a huge success in London (where it is still running), to a $17 million advance sale on Broadway. Other musicals on a grand scale produced in the less demanding financial climate of London include *Cats, Me and My Girl, Les Miserables,* and *Starlight Express*. However, *Carrie* followed the same route with disastrous results, and *Winnie* and *Zeigfeld* ran into too much trouble to think of traveling abroad.

The drawing shown here includes Michael Crawford in the weighty role as the Phantom. (When I first sketched him twenty years earlier in Peter Shaffer's *Black Comedy*, he was a juvenile.) Also from the British cast was Sarah Brightman, wife of *Phantom* composer Andrew Lloyd Webber, who threatened to stall the New York production until Actors' Equity allowed her to appear. A compromise was reached after much apprehension and Brightman, referred to by Lloyd Webber as The Voice, opened in the show only to be poorly received by the man from the *New York Times*. In fact, his unflattering comments on her looks probably discouraged her stay beyond a few months.

Andrew Lloyd Webber.
TheaterWeek 1988.

The Phantom of the Opera. L. to r.: Sarah Brightman, Steve Barton, Michael Crawford. *TheaterWeek* 1988.

Black Comedy. L. to r.: Geraldine Page, Peter Bull, Michael Crawford, Donald Madden, Lynn Redgrave.
New York Daily News 1967.

In the 1991 Persian Gulf War, Iraqi atrocities against Kuwaitis who resisted Saddam Hussein's occupation of their country were reported. A particularly heinous practice of the Iraqis was to dump the tortured corpse of a resister on the doorstep of his home and prevent his burial by the family. It's a taboo that goes back to the ancient Greeks, and is the subject of conflict in Sophocles' *Antigone*. In the play, Antigone is forbidden by King Creon to bury her brother Polynices, who was slain in the desert while fighting for the throne of Thebes. In the 1971 production at the Lincoln Center Repertory, Douglas Schmidt's set featured decrepit statuary of valiant warriors that suggested the battlefield decay offstage.

Antigone. Martha Henry, Philip Bosco. *New York Daily News* 1970.

THE UMBRELLA

That great actor Franchot Tone, though successful in Hollywood, returned frequently to the theater. In the few times I saw him at rehearsals, he was soused. In one instance, the play responsible, called *The Umbrella* by Frank Umberto and headed for off-Broadway via Philadelphia, was about mental patients acting out their fantasies in the asylum's junkyard. Others in the cast were Anthony Franciosa and one of my favorite actresses, Geraldine Page.

As I arrived, director Gene Frankel called for the start of Act Two. "Okay," said Tone, "We fucked up Act One; now let's fuck up Act Two," and what followed was an act of baffling non sequiturs, with Tone's profane asides continuing. I was embarrassed for Page, who was just a few feet away from me.

At every break, Tone went out for another drink, returning more unbuttoned than ever. Suddenly, Frankel called for a pause and sat in deep thought. "What are you thinking, Gene?" demanded the revved-up Tone. "I'm trying to figure the meaning of the scene," said Frankel. "Well, if the director doesn't know what the fuck it means, how in hell are the actors supposed to know?" And out he staggered for still more booze at the bar across the way.

As I rushed to complete my drawing for the *Philadelphia Bulletin* that evening, the show's press agent phoned and told me to hold up on the finish. I asked who replaced Franchot Tone and he was astounded at my information.

"How'd you know?"

"I was there today, so I know."

Anyhow, that's how Arthur O'Connell got into *The Umbrella*, which failed miserably out of town. A few years later a new production of *The Umbrella* did make it to off-Broadway but flopped once again.

As for Tone, he is seen here in one of his superb performances, that of Nina's father in the Actors' Studio production of *Strange Interlude*.

Strange Interlude by Eugene O'Neill. Franchot Tone, Geraldine Page, Rip Torn, Richard Thomas, and Pat Hingle. *New York Daily News* 1963.

The Umbrella. L. to r.: Anthony Franciosa, Arthur O'Connell, Geraldine Page.
Philadelphia Bulletin 1962. No photo call.

GRAND HOTEL

The drawing shown here of *Grand Hotel*, a 1990 hit musical, brings to mind a number of curios. First created as an illustration for the Drama Desk yearbook, the drawing was reproduced later on the invitation to my exhibition, and subsequently sold to a collector. More important, I sketched Michael Jeter in his prize-winning role as Kringelein having a last fling with Jane Krakowski, the secretary who wants to make it to Hollywood.

After the normally difficult career as a journeyman actor with an alcohol problem, Jeter made the most of his big opportunity in *Grand Hotel*, in which he was called upon to dance, though he had absolutely no experience as a dancer! Choreographer-director Tommy Tune didn't let that fact bother him. He simply asked Jeter to dance as he saw fit and developed his movements, expanding his capabilities into the show-stopping performance that resulted in glowing reviews.

Some twenty years earlier in Los Angeles, authors Wright and Forrest, usually identified with musicals based on the tunes of composers like Grieg and Borodin (*Song of Norway*, *Kismet*), landed Hollywood star Paul Muni for the same role that later made Jeter. *Grand Hotel* was then called *At the Grand*, and Muni was returning to the stage for the first time since *Inherit the Wind*, in which he portrayed the colorful attorney Clarence Darrow at the Scopes trial. Muni came on as a legend, giving top-heavy consideration to his role, experimenting with makeup and a range of acting styles. The production did not jell, but a startling situation having to do with the easy-going backstage life did develop. The large cast included many scantily clad chorines who visibly shocked Muni, and that was all they needed. Many of the girls, including star Joan Diener, "flashed" for him at every opportunity, resentful that he was demoralized with the show. He quit as soon as possible. Without him, *At the Grand* canceled the Broadway engagement despite a sizable advance sale. The 1990 version was extensively reconceived.

Grand Hotel. Jane Krakowski and Michael Jeter. 1990.

NEW FACES

Another director who surpassed his cast's performance was Leonard Sillman as he readied another edition of *New Faces*. One of my out-of-town newspapers, the *Toronto Star*, asked me to sketch the show for its opening in Toronto.

At the rehearsal I was able to catch a few indifferent numbers before Sillman called his cast together to tell them he was unhappy with them. In fact, as matters now stood, he suspected they were preparing a group suicide. I sat spellbound as he launched a performance worthy of John Barrymore.

"An artist has come all the way down from Toronto to sketch you" (His facts were a little mixed up here!) "—and you are a disgrace! I have staked my reputation on you. My thirty-year career in the theater hangs in the balance and a small fortune is on the line!"

Then he got down to examples. "When they see just how bad ———— is on opening night he'll be finished even on radio! And ———— is so worried about the size of her boobs, she can't dance! She'll never get another club date after we open! ———— has a father involvement that's choking up her voice and ———— has psychosomatic bellyaches. When the critics take one look at this bunch they will yell 'AMATEUR NIGHT!' " On he went, with indignant attitudes, dread silences, and flamboyant gestures, like the coach at halftime behind by three touchdowns.

Unfortunately, Sillman's worst fears were realized. The show was a fiasco, although several of the players survived, including Juan Carlos Copes and Maria Nieves, seen here in a whip dance. They had hoped to duplicate the immense popularity they had in Argentina, where they were a legend as a tango team.

New Faces of '62. Director Leonard Sillman is at right. The others l. to r.: Sylvia Lord, Jean Shepherd, Mickey Wayland, Patti Karr, Charles Barlow, Juan Carlos Copes, Maria Nieves. *Toronto Star* 1962.

A NIGHT IN VENICE

On a street celebrated for its colorful personalities, none was more striking than showman Mike Todd, best known for his hit Todd A-O film, *Around the World in Eighty Days*. His theatrical career started in the Chicago World's Fair in 1933 and he soon became identified with popular musicals and girlie shows. He refused to be typecast, however, and demonstrated his wider range of taste with productions of Romberg's *Up in Central Park*, Maurice Evans's version of the G.I. *Hamlet*, Moliére's *The Would-Be Gentleman*, and Johann Strauss's operetta *A Night in Venice*.

I attended rehearsals of the latter production in the new Jones Beach Marine Theater, where Todd stood high in the grandstand, waving his oversized cigar as he encompassed the sprawling event. There was a wide moat between the seats and the stage; perfect for Strauss's haunting "Lagoon Waltz." Three ornate sets rotated on an enormous turntable beyond.

Todd welcomed me warmly, as usual, and told me to roam freely over the temporary bridge to the stage and sketch away as the cast performed.

Later, during a break in the action, he approached and spoke to me in confidence. "Don't look now, but do you see that lovely blonde girl over there in the blue leotard, having the Coke? Sketch her and I'll do the rest." This I proceeded to do and soon Todd stalked over and demanded, "Whom are you sketching, that one? No, don't draw her, do someone else!" And he pointed to the right.

I don't know whether his womanizing strategy worked, only that he had amusingly made me part of it.

A Night in Venice. Michael Todd, right, impresario of the spectacular, communicates with the stage from the grandstand as some of his cast of 500 rehearse at 8000-seat Marine Stadium in Jones Beach, where the extravagant adaptation of the Johann Strauss opera opens Thursday night. *New York Compass* 1952.

Michael Todd's Peep Show, the hit revue at the Winter Garden, contains a mad and funny travesty of T. S. Eliot's "Cocktail Party," staged by comic Bobby Clark. Clark mixes lunatic paperhangers, burlesque funnymen and lots of dames. The bearskin rug can't stand it and flies away. Burlesque Comics: Red Marshall (receiving selzer from) Hi Wilberforce Conley, while Peanuts Mann works the liquor. *New York Compass* 1950.

Although I am known as a sketcher of the theater, I have drawn every form of entertainment I can think of, even the creation of a porn movie. To the best of my knowledge, however, the drawing seen here is the only one of the rodeo. I decided to sketch the star of the show, Doug "Droopy" Brown, in action and use the occasion to make a study of his enraged mount.

He appreciated the result and sent word through the press agent that he wanted to purchase the original art. He left a number. I was told he'd just checked out. He then phoned me directly. I was away on vacation. After several months of missing each other, he showed up at my studio with money. As I pulled out that drawing to wrap it, he said, "Hold on! I thought it would be small, just like in the paper," obviously unfamiliar with the reduction process. "That's about a foot and a half tall! Much too large to tote around to hotel rooms. I have no home of my own. I'm really sorry about that." And he left.

All I could think about was the unique way I had lost a sale.

Rodeo. World champion bullrider Doug (Droopy) Brown.
New York Daily News 1970.

In Hy Kraft's comedy *Cafe Crown* (revived recently), a nostalgia piece about the all-but-vanished Yiddish theater, Hymie the waiter invests in shows as a sideline. But he turns down a bid to buy into a production of *King Lear* stating, "As a writer Shakespeare had talent, but on the stage he's a flop. I put a bundle into Richard, One, Two, Three. Never again!"

Hymie was observing a fact; few Shakespearian revivals have enjoyed long runs or substantial profits.

A notable exception was an excellent production of the then rarely presented *Richard II* in the late thirties, starring Maurice Evans. Richard Burton led a big-name cast in *Hamlet* in the sixties, and if the stage door crowds did not have enough to wait for, Burton's wife, Elizabeth Taylor, arrived almost nightly to escort Richard home.

Much excitement was generated for The Bard during the 1990 season when Dustin Hoffman brought his successful London performance as Shylock in *The Merchant of Venice* to Broadway, selling out a three-month limited engagement. The production was marked by literal acts of expectorating as per Shylock's early complaint by Antonio, "You spit at my Jewish gabardine."

In the two instances I witnessed, the audience gasped in shock. When critic John Simon saw it he referred to it as a three-and-a-half-spit version.

A 1964 production of *The Merchant* had George C. Scott playing Shylock as seen here. Below, I depicted the opening of the new permanent Delacorte Theater in Central Park, in which it ran for several weeks.

The sketch reminds me of Joseph Papp's pivotal struggle with Parks Commissioner Robert Moses to acquire the facility, which has presented New York Shakespeare Festival summer productions ever since. It also represented a rare defeat for power broker Moses, who demolished entire neighborhoods to run his highways through the city, bulldozing popular resistance along with buildings.

In this case, his right-hand man persuaded Moses that Free Shakespeare ought to go. It was bad for the grass and it encouraged homosexuals. Moses prevailed on the city fathers, including then-Mayor Robert F. Wagner. Trial balloons of official plans to drop Free Shakespeare floated over the town. Indignant fans came to the rescue, including Nathan Handwerker, owner of "Nathan's Famous" hot-dog chain. Handwerker offered Papp free space in his large parking lot at his suburban Oceanside branch near Atlantic Beach.

For some this seemed worth considering but the indomitable Papp's only response to Handwerker was, "I love Nathan's hot dogs." He then turned the heat on the New York city council, where he rallied so much support that Robert Moses reversed himself and actually became very cooperative in constructing the new stadium-type theater. Soon the city council also granted a building and appropriation for what became the permanent year-round theater complex on Lafayette Street.

The Merchant of Venice. L. to r.: Geraldine James (Portia), Dustin Hoffman (Shylock), Basil Henson (Duke of Venice). *Stages* 1990.

The Merchant of Venice. Nan Martin, George C. Scott. New York Shakespeare Festival in Central Park. 1962.

DUSTIN HOFFMAN AS WILLY LOMAN

Although Lee J. Cobb had a lengthy and varied career, none of his roles could equal the stature he attained as Willy Loman in Arthur Miller's *Death of a Salesman.* His performance became the yardstick by which other Willys were judged.

Thus it was with skepticism that many greeted the announcement that the slight Dustin Hoffman would play a part where Cobb's corporeal size had become identified with the role.

Miller himself had no such doubts because his original concept of Willy was that of a little guy, and it had changed only because Cobb auditioned so well.

Hoffman once again gave proof of his versatility and triumphed in his version as the salesman. Many in the theater community were therefore stunned when that year's Tonys did not even nominate him for the acting award. The Drama Desk did give him their plaque for outstanding actor, however, and in his acceptance speech, Hoffman, taking note of the presence of Robert Prosky in the audience (receiving an ensemble acting award for *Glengarry Glen Ross*), quoted Arthur Miller as having called Prosky the best Willy Loman since Cobb when he performed it a couple of years earlier at Washington's Arena Stage.

Dustin Hoffman as Willy Loman in *Death of a Salesman.* *New York Daily News* 1985.

THE SEA HORSE

BY JAMES IRWIN

In 1974, a play called *The Sea Horse*, presented by the Circle Repertory, then a fast-rising off-Broadway company, won a Drama Desk award as an outstanding new play. Conchata Ferrell and Edward J. Moore, its cast of two, portrayed a stormy courtship. Ferrell was cited for her acting.

In accepting his award, the playwright turned out to be the actor in the play, who used an author's pseudonym just in case the critics didn't like his play. Now that they did, he was able to come out of the closet and declare himself the author. The Drama Desk promptly gave him another award certificate with his true name on it.

The Sea Horse. Circle Repertory. Conchata Ferrell and Edward J. Moore.
New York Daily News 1974.

Sleuth. Keith Baxter, Anthony Quayle (the sailor is a dummy). *New York Daily News* 1970.

Incidentally, with the economic squeeze affecting the theater in our time, there are some producers who will only finance plays with casts of one or two, preferably on a single set. One successful example is seen here: the virtuosic thriller *Sleuth*, with Keith Baxter and Anthony Quayle. (The sailor at right is a puppet.) Another, more recent hit is *Oleanna*, subject of heated controversy on the issue of sexual harassment.

Inversely, I have a special love and nostalgia for the plays in which George S. Kaufman collaborated. His casts were large and varied. The plays were usually in three acts. The end of Act Two had all hell breaking loose. Just when you were getting familiar with the entire cast, he surprised you in Act Three with a new character, who was even funnier.

Oleanna. Rebecca Pidgeon, William H. Macy. *Stages* 1992.

George S. Kaufman.

You Can't Take It With You. APA Repertory. L. to r.: Donald Moffat, Sydney Walker, Joseph Bird, Jennifer Harmon, Keene Curtis, Dee Victor, Clayton Corzatte, Kathleen Widdoes. *New York Daily News* 1966.

When a show is in trouble during its out-of-town tryout, the producer is faced with several choices. There are the usual repairs to be made on the score, text, or cast. A new director may be summoned, sometimes surreptitiously as a "doctor." More time may be needed and, if financing is available, the pre-Broadway tour is extended. Finally, if the outlook is truly bleak, the producer may decide to close his show in the provinces rather than subject it, and his own reputation, to the onslaught of the New York critics.

In 1958, Richard Ney, movie actor married to Greer Garson, produced a new musical named *Portofino*. Set on the Italian Riviera, replete with fine costumes and scenery, it found itself in difficulty in Philadelphia, where my drawing appeared with it. The local critics were bewildered by its inconsistencies, and the authors made radical story line changes without success. At last, when all hope was lost, Ney, a fine gentleman, called his cast together and left the decision to them. "Do we open in New York and hope for a long shot at some approval or do we close here?" The vote was overwhelming to go to Broadway for another week of work. The New York critics were merciless. It was Richard Ney's first and last production.

Portofino. Robert Strauss, left and right, as a friar and the devil. Center: Helen Gallagher and Georges Guetary.
Philadelphia Bulletin 1958.

GOLDEN BOY AND THE PHILADELPHIA BULLETIN

For years I enjoyed a happy relationship with the *Philadelphia Bulletin*. Occasionally the *Inquirer* would convince the New York press agent to favor them instead of the *Bulletin* with my advance drawing. Naturally, I liked being the center of the competition.

There were, however, two snags I hit with the *Bulletin*. One involved Sammy Davis, Jr., at the height of his stardom in *Golden Boy*, a musical

based on Clifford Odets's play. For the tryout in Philadelphia, I sketched Davis's heroic size as the contending boxer in the ring, surrounded by others in the cast.

The *Bulletin*'s drama editor phoned me on receipt of the art, saying that he could not use it in this form because the black star was too big. It might offend too many Philadelphians. Could I cut Davis down in size?

I would have loved to tell him right then and there what I thought of his appraisal of Philadelphians, but I had the show itself to consider. I called the press agent for advice. He suggested I make another drawing for the *Bulletin* as requested. He then enlarged the first one billboard size for the front of the New York theater, where it was seen for the lengthy run of the show.

Golden Boy. Center: Sammy Davis, Jr. The others, l. to r.: Charles Welch, Ted Beniades, Roy Glenn, Paula Wayne, Billy Daniels. Used on Majestic Theater billboard 1964.

The Good Soup. L. to r.: Sam Levene, Diane Cilento, Ruth Gordon, Jules Munshin. Pre-Broadway tour 1960.

The second incident involved a risqué play called *The Good Soup*, translated from the original French. The farcical staging had a hilarious piece of business where Sam Levene literally leapt into bed with Diane Cilento the minute her husband left the house. This is the scene I sketched. Again the *Bulletin* objected; this time on the grounds that this was a family newspaper and my drawing was obscene. The *Bulletin* did not print the drawing, but the somewhat broader minded *New York Daily News* did, for the Broadway opening. News editor John Chapman's maxim was: if it happens in the play, you can sketch it. But that was long ago. I'm sure that his standards would have been altered by much that has been heard and seen on stage in the years since.

Smith and Dale, those renowned comic vaudevillians, worked together for over sixty years and perfected their "Doctor Kronkite" medical sketch to the point that *New York Times* critic Brooks Atkinson begged them never to change it. I was privileged to see them play it in the early forties.

Smith was the patient, awaiting Dr. Kronkite. Dale, the doctor, comes waltzing in waving a handkerchief and introduces himself.

"I'm Dr. Kronkite."

"I'm dubious," says Smith.

"Pleased to meet you, Mr. Dubious. What is your trouble?"

"Doctor, every time I eat I lose my appetite."

Hearing this line, my wife responded as though she had heard the most hysterically funny comment of her life and led an audience of two thousand in uncontrollable laughter. To appreciate what happened, you would have had to witness her tepid response to some of the universally acclaimed jokes of that period.

Such was the effect of Smith and Dale.

The time came when Neil Simon wrote *The Sunshine Boys*, a play based on such a vaudeville team. In his play, the comics are coaxed out of retirement to do their Doctor routine for a television special.

The only trouble is their intense dislike for each other personally, and at the close of Act One the rehearsal ends in a fiasco of bickering at the very first line and the television show is canceled.

Aha, I thought. That's how Neil Simon sidesteps the impossible task of creating another "Doctor Kronkite" sketch.

I was quite wrong. In Act Two, to my amazement, Simon did devise his own, all-new Doctor sketch, convincing his audience that his old troupers were indeed screamingly funny.

Smith and Dale. The Doctor Kronkite sketch. "Laugh, Town, Laugh." *New York Herald Tribune* 1943.

The Sunshine Boys. L. to r.: Lewis J. Stadlen, Frank Albertson, Sam Levene. *New York Daily News* 1972.

THE HOSTAGE

The Hostage, a play set during the 1920 Irish Revolution, was probably Brendan Behan's most successful production. A company was formed for a national tour and I was asked to sketch that troupe at a rehearsal, for its promotional drawing.

Everything was normal until Helene Carroll blew a line, as follows: "And him boastin' what a hero he was, and how the town raised an erection to him in 1916." The entire cast cracked up for five minutes and poor Helene was embarrassed to tears.

The Hostage. National Tour. Helene Carroll at table with Donald Moffat. Above, l. to r.: Aubrey Morris, Victor Spinelli, Gwynn Edwards. Foreground unidentified. *Philadelphia Bulletin* 1961.

Borstal Boy, another Behan play, is an autobiographical story about a seventeen-year-old Irish youth on a mission to deliver bombs to the IRA in London.

I had to sketch this one at a sold-out preview and the best seat the management could offer me was in the rear. Not even my trick of holding the sketch pad on an angle to the stage light helped, because there was hardly any light from that source. The drawing seen here was sketched entirely from memory after the performance. No photos were available.

Borstal Boy. Niall Toibin as the mature Brendon Behan. Frank Grimes plays the teenage Behan. *New York Daily News* 1970.

Another play dealing with the Irish Rebellion. *Shadow of a Gunman*, O'Casey's first play. L. to r.: William Smithers, Susan Strasberg, Gerald O'Loughlin. *New York Daily News* 1958.

THE WISTERIA TREES

In 1950 Joshua Logan, fresh from his great success as director and co-author of *South Pacific*, threw himself into another project. His free adaptation of Chekhov's *The Cherry Orchard* was set in a similar time and social sphere but transferred to Louisiana. He titled it *The Wisteria Trees* and called upon his friend Helen Hayes to play the elegant lady who loses her estate (Hayes's daughter had recently died of polio and Logan was applying work therapy to divert her. It turned out badly for him because the workload hurt his own health as a result.)

You will recall that *The Cherry Orchard* ends with the loyal eighty-seven-year-old servant, Fiers, forgotten and left behind to die as everyone departs the old mansion. Some people protested that a lady of Southern aristocracy would *never* abandon the old slave in this American version of the play.

The sad farewells of the last scene recalled a wrenching incident I experienced three years earlier, showing how such things can happen.

On my return from military service in 1946, I rejoined my wife and young son, residing together with my in-laws in a remote section of Brooklyn. I will spare you the details, but we had no telephone due to company shortages in that area. Housing options were even worse, so I approached my next-door neighbor, an elderly insurance man, as to whether I could receive phone calls on his line for a fee. The kindly Mr. Gordon agreed, but declined compensation, and I was able to receive my assignments this way for over a year.

Then Mr. Gordon suddenly passed away and his widow sold the house, which included an apartment for her daughter's small family.

Their moving day came. Both households were packed by the movers for the trip to a one-family house some distance away in Flatbush, where they would all live together. The van took off and the family car was jam-packed with left-over items, looking like a bulging valise, with no room to spare. Mrs. Gordon told her son-in-law to meet the movers at the new place; she would follow by train, and besides, she wanted to mop the floors before the new owners arrived. He left.

When she was done, she paused outside for a last look at her house. Tired, overweight, sweaty, and disheveled, she made her statement: "When I came here forty years ago, I was a beautiful bride. My husband was handsome. This house was new. I was full of hope!" She turned and walked down the street toward the IRT station, carrying her mop and pail.

The Wisteria Trees. L. to r.: Kent Smith, Alonso Bosan, Walter Abel, Ossie Davis, Peggy Conklin, Bethel Leslie, Helen Hayes. *New York Compass* 1950.

PIPPIN

In the spring of 1972, I drove to Washington with my wife, Francie, to sketch the new musical *Pippin*, playing at the Kennedy Center. We stayed nearby at the Howard Johnson Hotel on Virginia Avenue, across from the Watergate apartments, which could be seen clearly from our room.

As we looked out the window, I remarked to Francie that Watergate housed the Democratic National Headquarters that had been broken into earlier that year.

Little did I know that in the months to come, it would be revealed that former CIA man E. Howard Hunt had monitored, from our very room, the Watergate break-in on the floor just opposite our windows.

Pippin proved a long-running hit in New York, with Bob Fosse's direction and choreography, Tony Walton's sets, Patricia Zipprodt's costumes, and striking performances by John Rubinstein, Ben Vereen, Leland Palmer, Jill Clayburgh, Eric Berry, and Irene Ryan. The show garnered several Tony and Drama Desk awards and nominations, particularly for Fosse and Vereen, whose careers took off from that point.

Another landmark was the highly effective television commercial, offering a glimpse of Fosse's twitchy dances. It hyped business and made television advertising mandatory for most musicals ever since.

But for me, *Pippin* will always be a reminder of the scandal that caused an American president to resign.

Pippin. Eric Berry, top. The others, l. to r.: Ben Vereen, John Rubinstein, Leland Palmer, Shane Nickerson, Jill Clayburgh. *New York Daily News* 1972.

ARSENIC AND OLD LACE

Although by the year 1941 my play-going experiences were just hitting stride, I had seen enough that when I attended *Arsenic and Old Lace*, I knew I was enjoying as funny a play as I was ever likely to see. Boris Karloff was cast as a psychopathic killer, a man who "looks like Boris Karloff." When his contract expired, he was replaced by Erich von Stroheim and the line was changed to a man who "looks like Erich von Stroheim."

His cringing foil was played by the gifted character actor Joseph Sweeney. When von Stroheim left the cast, Sweeney replaced him in a *tour de force* switch of roles. I was assigned to sketch him in both parts.

Arsenic and Old Lace. Joseph Sweeney, now playing the Karloff role of Jonathan Brewster, confronts Joseph Sweeney in his former role of Dr. Einstein. *New York Herald Tribune* 1943.

Arsenic and Old Lace, NBC television, stars Dorothy Stickney, Mildred Natwick, Boris Karloff, Tony Randall, and Tom Bosley (rear). *Philadelphia Bulletin* 1962.

Sweeney purchased the original and when I delivered it to his dressing room we chatted about the differences between Karloff and von Stroheim. The latter threw himself so totally into his role that when Sweeney tried to restrain his violence he sustained a hernia.

Twenty-one years later, while I was sketching NBC Specials for syndicated distribution, I finally had the chance to do Karloff recreating his original role for television.

The Cary Grant film had to wait in the can several years until the play ran its course on Broadway. While good enough to convey some of the original flavor, it did not approach the hilarity of the play.

After years of involvement with the work of Noel Coward as a happy member of his audience and in assignment to sketch his plays, the time came when I was asked to attend one of his rehearsals and come up with a version of the esteemed gentleman at work, for use in the out-of-town papers pre-Broadway.

The vehicle was *Sail Away*, which he composed, authored, and directed. The musical took place on a cruise ship. After he welcomed me to the theater lounge where the rehearsal was in progress, he became busily involved with book scenes of the various shenanigans that take place aboard such trips.

I sketched away as usual, but with added exhilaration at actually being in his informal presence, privileged to witness all those spontaneous suggestions and responses that are so revealing of a personality in unguarded conditions. After a half hour or so, lost in my work, I was happily surprised when he made a sharp turn and walked back to me to ask how I was doing. I showed him what I had, to that point, of him and his cast. He was amused, but had a suggestion: "Most caricaturists miss out on me because they don't give me enough *nose*. It's quite generous, you know."

"I'll watch it," I said.

With a pat on my back, he returned to his actors. Coward loved to draw and paint. In fact, he created the logo art for *Sail Away*. Though he was untrained and worked strictly as an amateur, his paintings were the subject of a well-hyped posthumous exhibition in London and offered for sale as high-priced souvenirs.

Sail Away. Noel Coward, foreground, oversees a rehearsal of his new musical. L. to r.: Grover Dale, Patricia Hardy, Jean Fenn, James Hurst, Elaine Stritch. *Boston Globe* 1961.

In the fall of 1961 I had occasion to sketch a rehearsal of a new play, *Daughter of Silence*, by Morris L. West, author of *The Devil's Advocate*, which was well received earlier.

Daughter dealt with a young girl on trial for the murder of the mayor of an Italian town. The girl was played by Janet Margolin, just out of her high school drama class, making her Broadway debut. In her one scene she was poignantly introspective and was then called upon to throw a harrowing fit. I remember her rushing off to her dressing room immediately afterward to recover.

That evening I called a close friend whose daughter I knew to be her classmate. I told her what I had seen and that perhaps Janet Margolin had a glowing future on the stage. I was informed that back in the Dramatics Workshop her classmates judged that "she couldn't act worth a damn!"

Margolin won a Theater World award for her performance and was kept reasonably busy on stage and in films, by Woody Allen and others.

In the drawing seen here, the judge at extreme right is the actor Allan Frank, another instance of my noting a friend's career in my drawings whenever possible.

Daughter of Silence. L. to r.: Emlyn Williams, Rip Torn, Janet Margolin. *New York Daily News* 1961.

It was with a sense of awe that I traveled to Stratford, Connecticut, in the late fifties to see Katharine Hepburn in rehearsal as Portia in *The Merchant of Venice* to Morris Carnovsky's Shylock.

I sketched the legendary actress through all the steps and corrections of the rehearsal process. When the session ended, I approached the backstage exit at exactly the same moment La Hepburn did. "Get any faces?" she asked, flashing her genial smile as I flipped through my pad. She hopped on her bike and rode off with a wave.

Hepburn is that modern rarity: a box office name impervious to reviews. Her public will attend, whatever the vehicle, especially on tour. She made a hit in her only musical, *Coco*, based on Coco Chanel, the Parisian couturiere. When she left the show, that fine French actress Danielle Darrieux replaced her but, alas, business declined. After a few months *Coco* closed. Hepburn returned to lead the show on a national tour and profits zoomed again!

Katharine Hepburn. *A Matter of Gravity.*

Katharine Hepburn and Robert Ryan in *Antony and Cleopatra. New York Daily News* 1960.
American Shakespeare Festival, Stratford, CT.

Katharine Hepburn as "Coco." From exhibition 1970.

Coco. Danielle Dardieux, center, as Coco Chanel. The others, l. to r.: Dan Siretta, Will B. Able, Robert Fitch, Chad Block. *New York Daily News* 1970.

For those who love the living theater, it is sufficiently gratifying if a new season offers us a dozen good plays with solid performances. Sometimes, without warning, we strike it rich. A great new play sends us into the night aglow! And rarer still, we are captivated by a stunning new personality, and this is even more exciting because now we may look forward to his or her future appearances.

I have been thrilled by several such discoveries, but two of them readily come to mind: Meryl Streep and Catherine Cox. In 1976 Streep first appeared on Broadway in a revival of *27 Wagons Full of Cotton*, a one-act play by Tennessee Williams. Her hot-and-bothered, earthy performance as the young wife of a Southern dirt farmer was as nuanced and effective as it could be. After intermission she switched completely, to a thirties office secretary in Arthur Miller's short play *A Memory of Two Mondays*.

Tennessee Williams's *27 Wagons Full of Cotton*. Tony Musante, with whip, hears Roy Poole praise the charms of his wife, Meryl Streep.

Music Is (Musical adaptation of *Twelfth Night*). L. to r.: Catherine Cox, Christopher Hewitt, Sherry Mathis. Above, l. to r.: David Sabin, Laura Waterbury, Joe Ponazecki, Daniel Ben-Zali. *New York Daily News* 1976.

On the way home I had to memorize what was a strange name to me. I made extravagant predictions for her future. You know the rest.

Later that year Catherine Cox made her debut as Viola in *Music Is*, a musical based on Shakespeare's *Twelfth Night*. With her slender grace and supple voice in disguise as Count Orsino's page boy, she was the most convincing actress I had ever seen in the role.

Although her career has not been as phenomenal as Streep's, she has continued to perform with charm and humor, receiving her share of acting awards.

Until a couple of decades ago, it was unthinkable for a Broadway show to open in New York without an out-of-town tryout. I was kept very busy going to rehearsals in New York City, the point of origin, to create drawings for the tune-up cities, like Philadelphia, Boston, and Washington.

Frequently I caught only a portion of the action, but if it was typical and included the lead players, I had enough for my purposes. After a few years of this, I noticed that the sampling, even if brief, left an impression on me that was borne out 95 percent of the time when I viewed the finished product back in New York weeks later.

I decided to document my impressions and keep notes. For quite a while my experiment worked; the rehearsal proved an advanced stage of production. The written words were now spoken by painstakingly cast actors. The missing sets and costumes seemed minor factors influencing overall quality.

One fine day I attended a rehearsal that put a stop to my foolishness for good. I arrived just in time for the start of Act Two of *Come Blow Your Horn*, the first play, a comedy, by a new writer named Neil Simon, who had a background as gag-writer for comics on radio and TV.

True, there was no audience in the theater. My notebook impression found it to be strident and for the most part unfunny. I wrote it off and planned to forget it if it returned to New York.

Return it did, and it was a smash, a hot ticket, establishing Neil Simon forever. I hastened to see it and find just where my perspicacity had gone astray. It was simple: A number of situations were established in Act One, which I had not seen, that triggered howls of laughter in Act Two. The very same appearance of Lou Jacobi at the front door of his sons' pad in Act Two, which meant nothing to me in rehearsal, was now a scream because all during Act One he vowed never to go there.

Incidentally, in the drawing shown here, Jacobi, a conventional Jewish father, fed up with his playboy sons, having no one to turn to, tells his troubles to a vacant chair. Lou borrowed this bit from his own father. One evening, his father, in town from Canada, caught his son's imitation of him in the show. Lou waited in his dressing room for his dad's reaction, expecting the worst.

"Well, Pop, what did you think of my performance?" he asked.

"You know, son, I've known men just like that!" he answered.

Come Blow Your Horn. L. to r.: Arlene Golonka, Lou Jacobi, Natalie Ross, Hal March. *New York Daily News* 1961.

OLIVER!
AND THE NEWSPAPER STRIKE

I had just delivered my drawing for the smash musical *Oliver!*, in which the youngster is taught by Fagin "you've got to pick a pocket or two," when a newspaper strike was announced. The artwork rested on the drama desk of the *Daily News*, unused for the duration.

This was no brief work stoppage. In fact, it dragged on for almost four months, enough for the Oliver to outgrow his part. The drawing seen here shows the new Oliver.

Incidentally, newspaper strikes have had strong effects on the theater. For example, during one lengthy stoppage, press agents prevailed upon the TV channels to assign coverage of shows. That's how the TV critics were born.

Another strike was ongoing when *Kismet* opened. By the time the newspaper critics panned it weeks later, it was established as a hit. It has had revivals and is currently in the repertory of the New York City Opera. Incidents like that tempt some producers to wish we could do away with critics.

Oliver! Paul O'Keefe and Clive Revill. *New York Daily News* 1963.

Kismet. Lincoln Center Revival. L. to r.: Richard Banke, Lee Venora, Alfred Drake, Henry Calvin, Anne Jeffries. *New York Daily News* 1965.

Incidentally, newspaper strikes have had strong effects on the theater. For example, during one lengthy stoppage, press agents prevailed upon the TV channels to assign coverage of shows. That's how the TV critics were born.

Another strike was ongoing when *Kismet* opened. By the time the newspaper critics panned it weeks later, it was established as a hit. It has had revivals and is currently in the repertory of the New York City Opera. Incidents like that tempt some producers to wish we could do away with critics.

Another casualty of a newspaper strike was my drawing of Meryl Streep and Raul Julia as the leads in *The Taming of the Shrew*, which played for several weeks at the New York Shakespeare Festival in Central Park.

The strike lasted almost four months, by which time the production had long since vanished.

Fortunately it eventually found its way into print several years later as one of a group of my drawings to illustrate an article on The Bard in *Theatre Communications* magazine, now known as *American Theater*.

The Taming of the Shrew. New York Shakespeare Festival 1978. Raul Julia, Meryl Streep. Not published because of a newspaper strike until used in *American Theater Magazine.*

Irving Berlin's 100th birthday in 1988 was cause for much celebration. Unfortunately "America's Tune King" hadn't been seen in public for many years and couldn't take part in the event. For this reason I felt fortunate to have seen this legend in action at his last Broadway show. During the summer of 1962 I was asked by the *Philadelphia Bulletin* to provide sketches of Berlin to go with an interview at a rehearsal of *Mr. President*. He turned out to be as active and extroverted as ever. He assisted Josh Logan in the direction and eagerly demonstrated how each number ought to go, like any other Tin Pan Alley song plugger. He shouted suggestions from the seats to Robert Ryan, Nanette Fabray, and Anita Gillette on the stage.

Although he was a highly regarded seventy-four-year-old at the time, it was just another interesting assignment for me. Today it is a valued memoir.

Irving Berlin at the *Mr. President* rehearsal. L. to r.: with authors Howard Lindsay and Russel Crouse. Robert Ryan, singing. Center: with director Joshua Logan, top, and Anita Gillette, below. Right: with Nanette Fabray. *Philadelphia Bulletin* 1962.

TEXAS TRILOGY

Early in the 1976 season, playwright Preston Jones, who had received extravagant praise in Washington, D.C., for his *Texas Trilogy*, a saga in which the life and times of a Southwestern family were conveyed during the course of three evenings, looked forward with heady anticipation to the Broadway opening that could prove to be the threshold of Recognition.

Unfortunately, the highly touted plays met little appreciation from Clive Barnes, the daily *New York Times* critic, and the expensive repertory presentation, unable to surmount that obstacle, closed after a short run.

The trilogy's director, Alan Schneider, commented during a Drama Desk panel that the British-born Barnes, lacking familiarity with Nehi soda pop or hominy grits, was in no position to enjoy the flavor of Jones's slice of Americana. In any case, Schneider added, his damaging opinion was yet another instance of the disproportionate entrenched power of the daily *New York Times* critic.

He therefore proposed that all theater critics be rotated, by paying each one $50,000 per year, after which time he would be shot.

Seated in the audience was Henry Hewes, theater critic of the *Saturday Review*. Intrigued by the idea, he rose and asked, "How about making that $75,000?"

Jokes aside, some time later the playwright died and Schneider confided to me that Jones, an alcoholic, had been unable to overcome his failure.

A Texas Trilogy. Left: *The Last Meeting of the Knights of the White Magnolia.* L. to r.: Paul O'Keefe, Graham Beckel, Henderson Forsythe, Thomas Toner, Walter Flanagan, Fred Gwynne. Center: *The Oldest Living Graduate.* L. to r.: Kristin Griffith, Lee Richardson, Patricia Roe. At right: *Lu Ann Hampton Laverty Oberlander.* Patrick Hines, Diane Ladd. *New York Daily News* 1976.

Sweeney Todd was a clear Tony and Drama Desk winner as outstanding musical for the 1978–79 season and received additional accolades in an intimate revival a decade later off-Broadway.

At a preview of the original Broadway version I was overwhelmed by director Harold Prince's startling effects. The somber tone was set as a gaunt organist, dressed like a chimney sweep, came slinking in to his keyboard and sounded his gloomy, foreboding chords. A girdered ramp bridged the stage overhead and men-aced everything beneath it as it ground and rotated to different positions. We were then treated to blood-spurting throat slittings, accompanied by screeching blasts from factory whistles. Next, Stephen Sondheim gave us a patter song, in the manner of a W. S. Gilbert gone mad, celebrating cannibalism, as Angela Lansbury described the wide selection of her human meat pies. In that preview an elderly judge stripped to the waist in a frenzy of self-flagellation to appease his lust for Sweeney Todd's young daughter. I left the theater stirred by what I had seen but doubtful that the critics or the public would accept it. How foolish of me to think they were any different.

It then became only a matter of time before Sondheim's penchant for mordant satire would surface again. Judging a showcase for new playwrights, he came across a play about presidential assassins. The idea intrigued him, although he felt the realization by the young author was not successful. He purchased rights to the idea, and with Jerome Weidman working on the book, he came up with a daring, scathing musical called *Assassins*. In it he gathered a group of assorted nuts and made an engaging, devastating study of their convoluted motives to achieve immortality while doing in a string of American presidents. Some critics, like John Si-mon, wished Sondheim hadn't selected such a project, especially with the Persian Gulf War raging, and would have given him a cigar if he had abstained. Doug Watt, in the *Daily News*, suggested a better idea would have been to do a show called *Mistresses*, a presidential common denominator with far richer entertainment potential. *Assassins* received enough praise after a limited off-Broadway engagement in New York to warrant a cast recording and regional and foreign productions.

Sweeney Todd. Angela Lansbury and Len Cariou. Above: Victor Garber, Sarah Rice, and Edmund Lyndeck.
New York Daily News 1979.

In 1990, controversy centered around Briton Jonathan Pryce rocked the theater world. The issues were 1) whether his award-winning performance in London was indispensible enough to preclude casting his role in *Miss Saigon* with an American actor in the Broadway version; and 2) whether the role, that of a Eurasian, should be played by an Oriental in any case. (Pryce had used tape on his eyelids, which was offensive to Asians.) The producers prevailed. Pryce opened to receptive critics and audiences, though sans tape, as seen here.

Jonathan Pryce in *Miss Saigon. Stages* 1991.

Comedians. L. to r.: Rex Robbins (with pencil), David Margulies, John Lithgow, Jeffrey De Munn, Larry Lane, pianist Woody Kessler, Jonathan Pryce, Jarlath Conroy, Milo O'Shea (at table). *New York Daily News* 1976.

In this drawing, Pryce appears in the 1976 play *Comedians*, for which he won a Tony Award. Directed with flair by Mike Nichols, the play was set in an English workingmen's club where amateur comics showcase their talents and reveal their personal problems. The actors were all so fine that I had to sketch the entire cast.

DECIBELS

Those of us who have found ourselves trapped in a disco, enveloped in an explosion of decibels, swirling lights, crackling lasers, and bouncing bodies, know that for some the scene can be a trial rather than a trip. I thought I was the only one whose ticker was about to lose out to that gigantic bass-reflex booming behind me, programmed to a common wavelength of sympathetic vibration—until I met many others similarly menaced at such events.

Sophisticated synthesizers and massive sound control consoles are now commonplace. Wires emanate from all musical instruments, many of which eliminate the traditional soundbox, leaving only a keyboard and a wire. Should the tune be the work of a self-taught kazoo artist, the words the breakthrough of an inarticulate, and the amplification in a state of feedback, the captive listener thinks only of a swift exit.

When souped-up electronics first hit in the fifties, John Chapman wrote in his review of an Eddie Fisher concert at the Winter Garden (where Al Jolson once filled the house without a mike) "The place was bugged like a tenement sink."

I remember a childhood experience in Madison Square Garden, before electrical amplification, where the singer used a megaphone à la Rudy Vallee.

Some years later I found myself immersed in classical music, flushed with the discovery of Jean Sibelius and with a newly issued first recording of his Fifth Symphony. As my Magnavox issued forth the wild discords of the first movement's development section, my father returned home suddenly and demanded to know what was wrong with the phonograph. Upon my explanation he branded the piece a lot of noise. Recognizing his seniority and his roof, I subsequently played such records in the basement.

To this day I cannot reconcile the deep pleasure of music with the possible offense to anyone unsympathetic. It takes care.

The ultimate fiasco befell a young musician I knew who was demonstratating a new recording to a cousin during a family get-together. The volume went up a bit to reveal some detail in the crowd scene at the fair in Stravinsky's *Petrouchka* ballet. The boy's father shouted from the next room to cut the volume. The boy complied, but minutes later Petrouchka's anger and frustration rose from the grooves and this time the enraged father burst into the room, grabbed the record and smashed it, ripped out the tone arm, and slammed the turntable to the floor. Then he stomped on it. The family was powerless to stem his overkill.

Some years later, the son took his life. He had been living alone, isolated from a family that had never acknowledged or accepted his homosexuality. In his will he left his modest savings to his only friend, a kindly lady next door. His father, an attorney, had the will declared invalid on the grounds of the suicide's mental incompetence, thus robbing his son of his last remaining expression of love.

Tommy. Michael Cerveris, pinball wizard. *Stages* 1993.

In 1977, a revival of the Kurt Weill–Bertolt Brecht 1929 musical *Happy End* opened on Broadway after originating at BAM's (Brooklyn Academy of Music) Chelsea Theater. The story line anticipated *Guys and Dolls*, in which a young Salvation Army lady reforms a group of gangsters. Meryl Streep, in the lead, wasn't quite ready for the Broadway opening so her understudy, Alexandra Borrie was pressed into service and it was she who appeared in my drawing.

When Borrie saw herself so aggrandized she complained to press agent Susan Bloch, who had thought she was doing the right thing by casting some limelight on a deserving performer.

This in turn reminded me of an incident described by producer Jean Dalrymple in her autobiography *September Child*. During her days as a press agent, she was engaged to publicize a Russian violinist, a contemporary of pianist Vladimir Horowitz (who had become a sensation on these shores while the violinist's career languished).

Dalrymple did her job well and when her client's next Carnegie Hall recital sold out for the first time, she went backstage just before the concert to celebrate with him. She found him the picture of Slavic despair, so she made sure he knew it was standing room only out front.

"Yes," he said, "Bot they are coming because of your pobleecity, not for me!"

That's when she knew you can't win 'em all.

I asked Jean to identify the ingrate for me and discovered him to be Nathan Milstein.

Happy End. Alexandra Borrie and Christopher Lloyd, center. Upper left: Donna Emmanuel, Prudence Wright Holmes, top; Christopher Cara, Joe Grifasi, below. Upper right: Grayson Hall, John A. Coe, Raymond J. Barry, top; Rob Weil, Tony Azito, below. *New York Daily News* 1977.

Macbeth

and Richmond Crinkley

Regimes at the Lincoln Center Theater, housed in the Vivian Beaumont, have always been burdened with problems extraneous to their productions, such as the payment of security and heating fees to Lincoln Center.

When Joseph Papp withdrew, Richmond Crinkley, producer of the successful *The Elephant Man* and *Tintypes*, formed a new company and, in November 1980, launched a season of three plays with *Macbeth*. Acclaimed opera director Sarah Caldwell came up with an unusual production that failed to persuade the theater critics. Caldwell is seen here in her former corpulence, presiding over the rehearsal with a mike from high up in the arena-style seats. (Those steep seats caused gout-ridden critic John Chapman to rebel. He arbitrarily sat himself down in the seats nearest the entrance door. Susan Bloch, the house press agent at the time, had to assign his review location to the patrons displaced.)

A revival of *The Philadelphia Story* didn't excite the critics either and a mildly funny play by Woody Allen, *The Floating Light Bulb*, completed the indifferent season. Crinkley blamed the theater and its poor facilities for his failure and demanded a four-million-dollar alteration from Lincoln Center before he could continue. After three years of haggling while the theater remained dark, Crinkley was outvoted and replaced by producer Bernard Gersten and director Gregory Mosher, who, using the existing plant, proved talented and lucky with a string of hits: *Anything Goes, The House of Blue Leaves, Our Town* (all revivals), and *Sarafina*, among others.

Sadly, Richmond Crinkley died at age forty-nine, before he could redeem himself in new ventures.

Sarah Caldwell directing *Macbeth* 1981.

Macbeth. Maureen Anderman, Philip Anglim. *New York Daily News* 1981.

The Elephant Man. L. to r.: Penny Fuller, Kevin Conway, Philip Anglim. National Tour 1979–1981.

Tintypes. Top: Carolyn Mignini, Jerry Zaks, Mary Catherine Wright. Below: Trey Wilson, Lynne Thigpen.
New York Daily News 1980.

No single person shaped the New York area more decisively than master builder Robert Moses. Though he was obviously too busy for such frivolities as the theater, he became involved in the construction of a number of them. These included two in which he took a personal hand: the Marine Theater at Jones Beach and the Aquarama at Flushing Meadow Park. His keen interest in them was no doubt influenced by the fact that he was a swimming champ in his youth. The Marine Theater was designed to exploit aquatic skills. Eight thousand spectators could observe feats performed from two concrete diving towers flanking the stage. A navigable lagoon separated that stage from the grandstand. When the theater opened in 1950, critic Brooks Atkinson remarked, "I had the best seat in the house up front, but I could scarcely see what was happening on that stage across the water."

The stage itself was a gigantic facility. Its turntable rotated three different sets. These were surrounded by a sweeping curved structure that could become anything from a Norwegian mountain range to a Manhattan skyline.

A tricky tunnel enabled swimmers to surface from the middle of the lagoon to perform in the water. A barge could set off a fireworks display behind the stage area. An actual seaworthy craft was used when *Show Boat* was presented there. Producer Guy Lombardo, a motorboat racer, made his nightly entrance to greet his audience in his personal launch. In *Song of Norway*, a barge bearing ice skaters sailed by.

To improve proximity, a stage was constructed on the lip of the grandstand, on the near side of the water. Ditto, the orchestra pit. The original stage still functioned across the water but was now connected by pontoon bridges on both ends. Exit and entrance cues changed from seconds to minutes as performers traveled the great distances.

Lombardo produced numerous musical revivals there through the years and was recognized with a special Drama Desk award for his efforts. I was curious as to his financial arrangement with the New York State Parks Commission but nobody ever gave a clear answer to my questions.

To this day I don't know whether the Marine Theater was solvent or subsidized.

Lombardo offered free dancing after the show as an extra attraction to his large beach audience. Louis Armstrong and his band were included among the musical artists.

Moses, in retirement in an old village in nearby Gilgo Beach, finally had time to attend the theater. His theater. He came to all the openings.

On one occasion I brought my mother from Brooklyn to Jones Beach when I had to sketch *Song of Norway*. Her experience was mainly with Yiddish theater and she could not understand why people would drive for an hour to a chilly beach just for a show. When the extravaganza was over she turned to me and thanked me for the best show she'd ever seen!

Over at Flushing Meadow, Moses placed a huge grandstand alongside a large swimming pool and producers were engaged to present shows there. I remember seeing a large casting ad in *Variety* for the first one:

AQUA CIRCUS IN
FLUSHING MEADOW!
BEAUTIES WANTED.
MUST BE EXPERT
DANCERS AND SWIMMERS.

One week later the ad was changed to:

WANTED!
GIRLS WITH GOOD FIGURES
WHO CAN SWIM.

(Note they are asked to forget about the face.)
Two weeks later:

WANTED!
GIRLS WITH GOOD FIGURES
WHO CAN SWIM A LITTLE.

The final talent show included a group of girls who didn't attempt to swim at all, but paddled their way about on surfboards! I captured these ladies in my drawing.

Not long after Lombardo's death, musicals were discontinued at Jones Beach. Today there are sporadic bookings of pop and rock events.

At the Aquarama we have just an abandoned pool with a lot of seats.

The Aqua Circus in Flushing Meadow Park. Top left: Los Argentinos, high diving champ in comic routine. Clown Rudy Docky. Below, left: a chimpanzee named Peanuts. Singer M. C. Jimmy Carroll. A girl in a plume dance and another in a Hawaiian surfboard routine. *New York Daily News* 1958.

Guy Lombardo's extravaganza *Mardi Gras!* at the Jones Beach Theatre, buttressed by Louis Armstrong and his band.
Guy and Louis and their bands will appear in each show, then play for dancing after the performances.
New York Daily News 1966.

Finian's Rainbow (Jones Beach). L. to r. top: Christopher Hewitt, Gail Benedict. Below: Ronn Carroll, Beth Fowler, Charles Repole, Stanley Grover. *New York Daily News* 1977.

Annie Get Your Gun (Jones Beach). L. to r.: Travis Hudson, Don Potter, Harve Presnell, Lucie Arnaz, Jack Dabdoub, Alan North. *New York Daily News* 1978.

MUNSTER AND SPOCK

The advent of television has solved the financial problems of countless actors. Those who land a successful series achieve the good life overnight, a tempting goal for people familiar with unemployment lines and all the attendant deprivations unknown by average wage-earners.

But eventually, most actors descend from the slopes of Beverly Hills in quest of nourishment for their souls, returning to their first love, the theater.

Waiting for them is an ambush of theater critics, seemingly eager to brand the invaders as hopelessly tainted by the sitcoms that made them Rich and Famous.

Usually this prejudice surfaces in conjunction with a flawed performance or poor choice of play. But sadly, many a fine actor will be victimized by quips—in particular Fred Gwynne of TV's *The Munsters* and Leonard Nimoy, *Star Trek*'s pointy-eared Spock. In tabloids like the *New York Daily News*, Gwynne is invariably the subject of headline puns relating to *The Munsters*, and most interviews, reviews, and stories on his theater work are apt to plague him with it as well. His version of Big Daddy in a revival of *Cat on a Hot Tin Roof* was so impressive that this fine production was moved from Stratford, Connecticut, to Broadway for a successful run. (At the memorial service for Tennessee Williams in 1983, playwright Jerome Lawrence told the following story: When his own play *Inherit The Wind* (which he wrote with Robert E. Lee) was trying out in Philadelphia, dyspeptic producer Herman Shumlin, nervous about its future, referred to the raves in New York for *Cat on a Hot Tin Roof* and asked, "Why don't *you* guys write a play about fucking?" Lawrence couldn't wait to quote Shumlin to Williams when they met soon afterward in Tangiers. His response: "Mr. Shumlin has it all wrong. *Cat* is a play about NOT fucking!")

Cat on a Hot Tin Roof. Stratford, CT. L. to r.: Charles Siebert, Joan Pape, Elizabeth Ashley, Fred Gwynne, Kate Reid, Keir Dullea. *New York Daily News* 1974.

Players. L. to r.: Tom Flagg, Rex Robbins, Fred Gwynne, Michael O'Hare, Thomas A. Carlin, Gene Rupert.
City News (a strike interim newspaper) 1978.

In the autobiographical play *Long Day's Journey Into Night*, Eugene O'Neill underscores the tragic choice his actor father made in purchasing performing rights to his hit play, *The Count of Monte Cristo*. While achieving financial security touring with it (including a summer home, the actual setting for *Long Day's Journey*, which he named Monte Cristo), he sacrificed the artistic rewards he might have enjoyed had he made more time for his acclaimed Shakespearean performances.

Which brings to mind two actors of our time who became similarly identified with hit roles. No role Yul Brynner played ever came close to his success in *The King and I*. And nothing Richard Kiley appeared in approached the reception given him for *Man of La Mancha*.

After his long run starting in 1949 as the King of Siam, Brynner made films, even a western, but never caught on. Brynner never abdicated the royal persona once he played the king and he behaved accordingly ever after. At one point he toured in a musical, *Odyssey* (originally called *Home, Sweet Homer*), in which I was asked to change my drawing to keep everyone else smaller than Brynner. (I had originally sketched a close-up of Joan Diener as Penelope on the right, for layout variety.)

Brynner eventually was compelled to revive and tour in *The King and I* to prove that all others who played the king were mere pretenders. He broke house records wherever it played and he died during its last run on Broadway.

Kiley, meanwhile, had a mild run in *No Strings*, Richard Rodgers's first solo attempt after the loss of his collaborator, Oscar Hammerstein II. He then tasted failure in a Lawrence-Lee play. He also starred in a forgotten musical, *Her First Roman*, with Leslie Uggams, based on *Caesar and Cleopatra*. (As is often the case, failed shows have been blessed with memorable decor; similarly, some of my favorite drawings have been for what turned out to be flops.) So Kiley returned to *Man of La Mancha* and knocked 'em dead again in a highly successful tour.

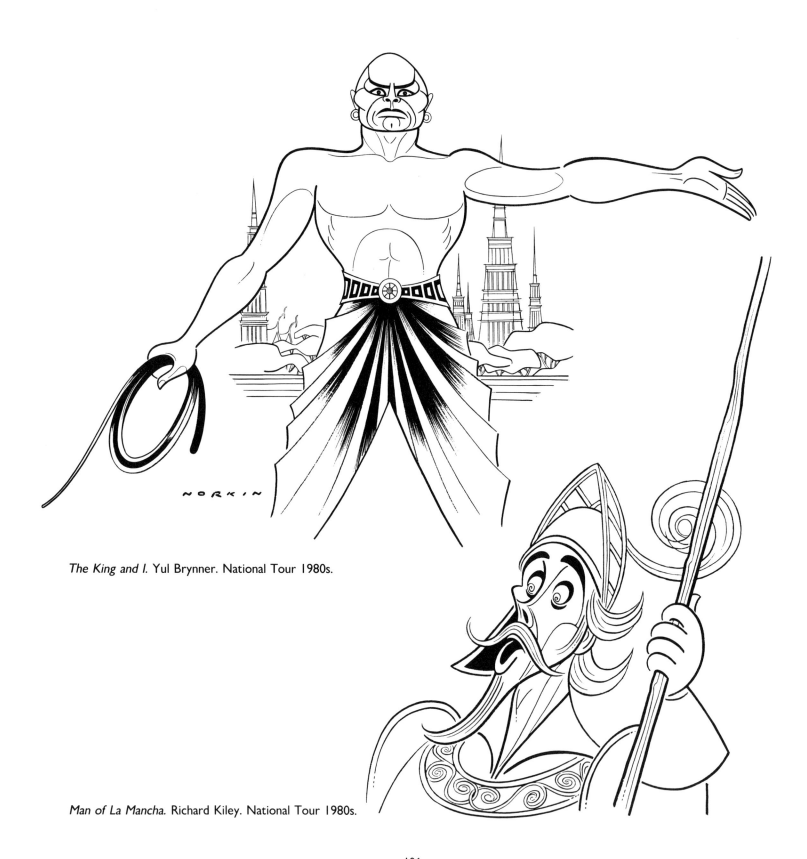

The King and I. Yul Brynner. National Tour 1980s.

Man of La Mancha. Richard Kiley. National Tour 1980s.

Home, Sweet Homer (later *Odyssey*). L. to r.: Yul Brynner, Diana Davila, Rusty Thatcher, Joan Diener.
Pre-Broadway tour 1975.

Odyssey (formerly *Home, Sweet Homer*). L. to r.: Rusty Thatcher, Yul Brynner, Diana Davila, Joan Diener.
New York Daily News 1976.

No Strings. L. to r.: Bernice Massi, Noelle Adam, Richard Kiley, Polly Rowles, Alvin Epstein, Diahann Carroll.
Toronto Star 1962.

Her First Roman. Leslie Uggams, Richard Kiley. *New York Daily News* 1968.

When *Applause* opened on Broadway, it signaled Lauren Bacall's arrival as a colorful baritone and a carefree dancer in a musical based on the film *All About Eve*. She was surrounded by a skilled cast, and in my drawing I took note of a featured dancer, a "gypsy" in the ensemble named Bonnie Franklin, who won a Theater World award (for newcomers) for that performance.

My next drawing of Franklin was for *Carousel*, a Jones Beach revival in which she sang the second lead.

Some ten years later, I heard from her agent. The formerly struggling actress, now a top TV star, wished to acquire the original artwork of my *Applause* and *Carousel* drawings.

Carousel. Bonnie Franklin and Reid Shelton. *New York Daily News* 1973.

Applause. Lauren Bacall, center. The others, l. to r., are Lee Roy Reams, Bonnie Franklin, Penny Fuller, and Len Cariou. *New York Daily News* 1970.

A Funny Thing

Theater history is spotted with rare but memorable cases in which out-of-town revisions turned a flop into a smash.

One such was *A Funny Thing Happened on the Way to the Forum*, which I found an unfunny bore in rehearsal. My sketch included a talented new actress named Karen Black playing the love interest. She was fired in Washington (allegedly because of her poor singing), flew to Hollywood, and quickly became a star.

Jerome Robbins was called in to redirect during the tryout and developed an extended introductory musical sequence to replace a brief, spoken one. It was called "Comedy Tonight," a hit number so charming and funny that together with the inflection he gave the humor throughout, critics and audiences were captivated when it opened on Broadway.

A Funny Thing Happened on the Way to the Forum. L. to r.: John Carradine, Karen Black, Zero Mostel, Jack Gilford, David Burns, Ron Holgate. *The Washington Star* 1962.

THE GOOD DOCTOR AND CHAPTER TWO

I was asked by my organization, the National Cartoonists Society, to put together a "Theater Night." As befitting such an occasion, I came up with an idea to honor a master of comedy, Neil Simon, and surround him with the stars from his hit plays. The actors proved only too happy to come to Sardi's for the event, which took place in early October. Some were seeing "Doc," as he is known to his friends, for the first time since the loss of his wife a few months earlier. Thus it was a surprise to Art Carney, Lou Jacoby, Maureen Stapleton, Jack Gilford, Carole Shelley, Jerry Orbach, Larry Haines, Marcia Rodd, Christopher Plummer, Tom Lacy, and Lee Meredith to see him arrive, beaming, accompanied by Marsha Mason, a soon-to-be-recognized fine actress. Mason was featured in *The Good Doctor*, an evening of several Chekhov stories dramatized by Simon and in rehearsal at the time.

Chapter Two. L. to r.: Judd Hirsch, Anita Gillette, Anne Wedgeworth, Cliff Gorman. *New York Daily News* 1977.

The Good Doctor. L. to r.: Christopher Plummer, Marsha Mason,
Rene Auberjonois. *New York Daily News* 1973.

In his acceptance speech for a plaque, Simon confessed that he might have been eligible for membership in our society had he succeeded in his original ambition: to write gags for cartoonists. He failed at it and eventually turned to television, stage, and films. When asked if his plays were autobiographical, he replied that *all* his experiences and observations were utilized. In fact, he was planning to sell this evening's event to Paramount.

He then let us in on a scoop: He had just met a most wonderful young lady, and this was the reason for his euphoria. He introduced a blushing Marsha Mason. Two weeks later they were married. The ensuing guilt over his sudden-found happiness became the subject of his next play, *Chapter Two*.

The drawing here appeared when Rock Hudson, former movie star known for his romantic comedy roles, was touring in *Camelot* in 1977.

After his tragic death, his biographer revealed that the high point in his career came when the *Variety* critic cited his performance in *Camelot* as marking a new hitherto unrevealed dimension as a serious actor.

Camelot. L. to r.: Jerry Lanning, Sherry Mathis, Rock Hudson, Iggy Wolfington. *New York Daily News* 1977.

If a movie star remains popular long enough, a crossroad is reached and a change has to be considered. The star must acknowledge the aging process and switch to more suitable roles or think about retiring. Then too, there is television. Finally, the star may do a play.

In 1952, the legendary Bette Davis did just that. In fact, the vehicle was a musical revue called *Two's Company*, and Davis sang in it. I was asked to design a logo caricature. I had created a number of them for various shows, but this was the first time a caricature of mine was made into a huge neon sign and placed above the marquee. The all-use deal also provided for its appearance in ads, and posters and on the cover of the playbill.

The show itself was a mixed bag that failed to enchant the critics. A curious public flocked to see Miss Davis in person for the first time. Then she went and took sick. A jaw operation was necessary and that was the end of Bette Davis on stage or anywhere, for a while.

Davis recovered nicely, returning to films in character parts and on stage again in Tennessee Williams's *The Night of the Iguana.*

Then, many years later, John Springer, promotion man turned producer, presented Davis in a one-person show. She toured in it and eventually played it in London, where she was warmly received.

Davis remembered my *Two's Company* logo and Springer tracked it down in the files of Artcraft, a theatrical poster company, for use in the new one-person show. I had signed the caricature originally but artists' names are apt to be stricken from their drawings in ads unless they provide for it contractually or are prepared to sue. Thus, my logo appeared, cloaked again in anonymity.

In England, EMI issued an LP recording, *Miss Bette Davis*, with my caricature the full size of the cover. The star even signed copies of the album for fans in the record shops. I saw the record album in the film *Outrageous*, used as part of the story. I acquired the recording in a New York shop and discovered that the cover design was credited to an artist named "Feref." I engaged a lawyer to investigate, starting with EMI records. I never witnessed a sleazier game of buck-passing. Since it was not that big a deal to warrant international pursuit, I turned to John Springer in New York. He explained how it all happend and said he would arrange for his producing partners, Columbia Artists, to make token restitution to me for Davis's use of the logo when performing, but since he had nothing to do with the recording, he could not help me there.

I should have known that such misappropriations were possible, since years earlier, during the run of *Two's Company*, I saw my logo baked on a porcelain ashtray in the window of The Show Shop, a souvenir store on West 44th Street. I happened to know the owner, who explained in all innocence that since there was no signature on it she thought it was sort of public domain. Hers was a business struggling to survive so she gave me an ashtray as a token of indemnity. I still have it to remind me of Goldwyn's maxim: A verbal agreement isn't worth the paper it's written on. Protect your signature in writing!

The
PLAYBILL
for the Alvin Theatre

TWO'S COMPANY

The Night of the Iguana. L. to r.: Margaret Leighton, Alan Webb, Patrick O'Neal, Bette Davis.
New York Daily News 1961.

Bette Davis caricature for exhibition ad, Guild Hall, East Hampton, NY c. 1975.

GIELGUD AND RICHARDSON

Sirs Ralph Richardson and John Gielgud won praise for their absorbing interplay as two mental patients in *Home*. On introducing them at a Drama Desk panel, critic George Oppenheimer said he felt like a rook, seated between the two knights.

Richardson confided that originally he was concerned by the play's lack of conflict, substance, or the sense of anything happening, so the critics' positive reception of the performances was a happy surprise.

In one scene Gielgud wept real tears. I asked him how he managed to cry on cue. He replied, "I think of something, but I won't reveal what it is."

Home. L. to r.: Ralph Richardson, John Gielgud, Mona Washburn, Dandy Nichols. *New York Daily News* 1970.

No Man's Land. L. to r.: John Gielgud, Michael Kitchen, Ralph Richardson, Terence Rigby.
New York Daily News 1976.

The School for Scandal. John Gielgud and Ralph Richardson. *New York Daily News* 1963.

There is one issue that guarantees heated disagreement among otherwise harmonious lovers of theater: nontraditional casting. Most minority actors demand the employment opportunities offered by it, while many audiences are puzzled by the suspension of disbelief demanded of them in the process. This does not apply to an all-black version of *Hello, Dolly!*, a lark in which the total novel transcription is anticipated by the audience. Contrast this with the ultimate goal of the nontraditionalists; color-blind casting, in which all wishes of the author will be ignored.

For me, the most serious consideration is the artistic. Nontraditional casting can be a fundamental threat to the magical effect of living theater; if you are passionate about that mystique you will find yourself enmeshed in heated disagreement with the nontraditionalists, who are just as committed to the cause of broadened employment opportunity.

A couple of cases come readily to mind. A 1974 revival of John Steinbeck's play, *Of Mice and Men* (from the celebrated novel), featured the great black actor James Earl Jones as the simple-minded Lenny. One of the ranch hands is a black named Crooks. He is ostracized and lives alone in the barn. In a key scene, Lenny visits him and, too lacking in guile to be prejudiced, treats him as an equal. Crooks is lonely and angry: "S'pose you didn't have nobody—'cause you was black. How would you like that?"

The entire point made by Steinbeck is lost if Lenny is also black.

Another serious instance of miscasting occurred in the 1975 revival of Arthur Miller's *Death of a Salesman*, directed by George C. Scott, who also played Willy Loman. In this production Willy's old friend and neighbor, Charley, and his son, Bernard, are cast as blacks. In a focal scene Willy visits Charley in his office for yet another loan. Charley gives freely but makes a repeated offer of a job, which Willy refuses: "I can't work for you. That's all, don't ask me why." If Charley is black, we assume that Willy's unspoken motive is racial prejudice, when the author's actual reason is the very basis of the play: a supposed superiority over Charley by Willy's imagined charisma. This is even extended to their sons. Willy's boy, high school sports hero Biff (now a failure), over seemingly inferior Bernard, Charley's son, a nerd who at this point is an attorney about to argue a case in the U.S. Supreme Court! "What's the secret?" asks a bewildered, self-deluded Willy Loman.

That self-delusion, "a smile and a shoeshine" spells success, is what Arthur Miller was writing about, with a fervor that struck a disturbing chord in audiences ever since. It is definitely not a play about racial prejudice, which is what nontraditional casting made of it.

Death of a Salesman. L. to r.: Ramon Bier, George C. Scott, James Farentino, Teresa Wright, Harvey Keitel.
New York Daily News 1975.

Of Mice and Men. L. to r.: Kevin Conway, James Earl Jones, Mark Gordon, Pamela Blair.
New York Daily News 1974.

HAROLD CLURMAN

The cold war between the Soviet Union and the United States lasted so long that some younger people don't realize that we were on the same side in World War II. While we were stemming Japanese advances in 1942, the Russians finally blunted the Nazi salient at Stalingrad in the bloody turning point of the European theater. No less an American leader than General MacArthur declared: "The fate of civilization rests on the banners of the Red Army!"

In this setting, a Soviet play, *Counterattack*, was made welcome on Broadway in 1943. It was a melodrama in which a Russian fights drowsiness as he awaits relief while holding off a squadron of Nazis momentarily trapped with him in a basement during a raging battle.

Encouraged by *Counterattack*'s reception, Harold Clurman, long associated with the Group Theater, directed another Soviet play, *The Russian People*. He aimed for the leisurely pace of Russian films and this play did not fare nearly as well with the critics as *Counterattack*. Clurman returned three weeks after the opening for a look at the play and was shocked to find that his cast, with an ear to the reviews, had sped up the pace. He called a backstage meeting and commanded his actors to return to his original concept: "If this play is to fail it's going to fail *my* way, not *yours*!"

In fact, Clurman maintained that an important factor on the road to artistic success was the "right to fail." Creativity is stillborn if we are guided only by the traditionally, commercially "safe."

For this reason his stay in Hollywood was brief. He scoffed at material success. "How many fine houses can I occupy? How many Cadillacs can I drive? How many suits can I wear?"

Counterattack. Morris Carnovsky, Rudolf Anders, Barbara O'Neill, and Sam Wanamaker. *New York Herald Tribune* 1943.

The Member of the Wedding. Carson McCuller's play has Julie Harris, center, as a twelve-year-old who has bought a fancy red gown. The others are Brandon De Wilde, left, and Ethel Waters. *The New York Compass* 1950.

LOST IN YONKERS

In Neil Simon's 1991 play *Lost in Yonkers*, two teenage boys placed temporarily in the home of their forbidding grandmother are unprepared for a series of family events that they come to witness. Frank Rich, in his *New York Times* review, felt that Simon had missed the chance to write a greater play by making the jolting grandmother-aunt problem merely one of many observed by the boys. The Pulitzer Prize committee, however, thought the play good enough to award it Best Play of 1991.

For me, the author's approach is exactly what made it so theatrically gratifiying. The play served to recall a youthful experience of my own that took a similarly shocking turn.

A closely knit group of boys in Brooklyn, of which I was a member, usually concerned itself with games—softball, stickball, touch football, and the such—would pause annually for a side project. It was a nocturnal cherry-pick. The tree in question was over the back fence of one of our gang, Moe. The task had to be carried out after dark and involved scaling a seven-foot fence to trespass into the adjacent backyard, then climbing the tree to pick it in all its fecundity. This was not easy because there were five of us and each bore a Wearever pot or floorpail that resounded with each plunking cherry. Cracking branches also gave us away. Young Lindstrom, a college student whose family owned the property, was disturbed by the noise as he studied for an exam. Out he came on the back porch in the darkness to ask effetely, "Who is there?"

Our ringleader, Eli, blurted out, "Three guesses!" The jig was up and down we came with a crash, pots and all, clambering back over the fence and scattering in all directions.

We assembled next day at Moe's house to check whether we had become a police case. We were lucky this time and were able to laugh about it. Moe had an older sister, much older, named Addy. She was what we called a "bleached blonde" in those days. We kids did not dwell on such matters, but she dated shady characters and had a girlfriend, another faded flapper named Lottie, who seemed even more disreputable. They were both home and got a kick out of the previous night's big event.

Lottie had a suggestion. Her mother had a house with a cherry tree in the backyard and we'd be welcome to the harvest there.

Lost in Yonkers. L. to r.: Jamie Marsh (top), Danny Gerard, Mercedes Ruehl, Irene Worth.
Stages 1991.

But she didn't want more than two of us and selected Eli and me. We went, carrying our pots, with Lottie to her house a block away. She asked us to wait in the living room while she notified her mother of our plans.

Then we heard sounds of an escalating argument from the kitchen.

Lottie's mother was saying it was the Sabbath. "Tell the boys to go home and come back tomorrow." Lottie's temper boiled over at being overruled. With a fury that implied much more than cherries for neighboring boys, she inflicted thudding blows on her mother. I have never heard more unnerving sounds than the hoarse groans of pain from the old woman. After a while there were only squeaking sobs.

Lottie returned to us, stony faced, and said, "It's O.K. now. Let's pick the cherries. Follow me."

"No," we said. "Forget it." And we left.

Today I have a stand of four flourishing cherry trees in my garden but I'm still frustrated. The birds get to the cherries before I do.

Because the art of caricature is also the art of exaggeration, I'm frequently asked if performers are ever offended by my drawings. The fact is that I've had numerous complaints when an actor has been *left out* of a sketch. And although I have a reputation for being kind, I'm quite sure I've offended many. Very rarely, however, have I heard from the victims.

One striking case occurred when I heard from Michel Mok, press agent for the original *The King and I*, that the star of the show, Gertrude Lawrence, was miffed at my version of her in the drawing seen here. You will notice that she has what I call a "heavy" nose, not a long one. Otherwise, I felt that my concept of her was stylized and sympathetic.

But then Mok conveyed another serious complaint. Lawrence resented being "right to lefted"— meaning that even though I had placed her dominant at the right, the caption would have to mention that relative "nobody" (at the time) Yul Brynner first.

It had never occurred to me that this could be the source of a complaint. I apologized for the heavy nose but rejected the right-to-left beef on the grounds of artistic freedom. As for Yul Brynner, he proved so immense in the role that it not only made him a star, but after many revivals and a few thousand performances, a national institution.

The King and I. Yul Brynner and Gertrude Lawrence. *The New York Compass* 1951.

HARVEY SABINSON

A contemporary of mine, Harvey Sabinson, who is currently Director of the League of American Theater Owners and Producers, started as a theatrical press agent and distinguished himself as such. At one point he represented producer David Merrick, who had five or six productions running simultaneously on Broadway. Sabinson was a hero in World War II, when, as part of General Patton's spearhead into Germany, he manned a forward machine-gun position in a village basement as the enemy attempted to retake the town. He mowed down repeated waves of troops from his strategic position and the American advance held.

He didn't look like a hero in the postwar years; roly-poly in figure despite his heavy smoking. One day he went on a diet and he became the new skinny Harvey we've known ever since.

About fifteen years ago he offered his memoirs as a veteran press agent. His book was called *Darling, You Were Wonderful!* and was filled with the insider's experiences, dripping with Names and Shows. However, he omitted one of his funniest stories.

His partner for years was that crafty master of promotion Karl Bernstein, who was ahead by a generation of publicity wars. Bernstein had learned that show business was characterized by feast or famine. One season, hits; the next, flops. Boom or depression, it was prudent to keep expenses down.

At one point he rented space from a dentist. It was the extra operating room, a cubicle barely large enough for two desks and a filing cabinet. To enter you passed through the dentist's waiting room, stocked with dog-eared back issues of *The New Yorker*.

Bernstein wasn't feeling well and went for a checkup. After a thorough exam the doctor advised him to give up smoking; his lungs were not a pretty picture. "Doctor, I don't smoke," said Karl. "But my partner, Harvey, he smokes all the time!" That's how small his office was. Did I say this was funny? It took years, but today the secondhand-smoke hazard is commonly recognized with bans in the workplace, restaurants, etc.

When Bernstein announced his retirement, I asked him for his funniest story. During one of his big hits, the superstar, whom he refused to name, called him to her hotel suite with a problem: she wanted Bernstein to spike the ugly rumors in the columns that she was enmeshed in a scandalous relationship with another star. It was endangering their marriages and disgracing their children.

As the media wizard was mulling over his scant options, the bedroom door opened, and in walked the star she was denying, in quest of more scotch.

Harvey didn't include that one in his book either.

Following, some David Merrick productions, either successful or of special interest. Above, *Vivat, Vivat, Regina!*
Eileen Atkins, left, as Queen Elizabeth; Claire Bloom, right, as Mary, Queen of Scots. *New York Daily News* 1972.

The Roar of the Greasepaint—The Smell of the Crowd. L. to r.: Lori Cesar, Cyril Ritchard, Anthony Newley, Gilbert Price, Joyce Jillson (later known as a leading astrologist), and George Hirose (as Mao Tse Tung).
Washington Star, Boston Globe 1965.

Luther. Albert Finney in the title role.
Below: Peter Bull, selling letters of indulgence.
New York Daily News 1963.

Stop the World—I Want to Get Off. Author-director-star Anthony Newley. Anna Quayle, Jennifer and Susan Baker.
New York Daily News 1962.

Hello, Dolly! (Westbury Music Fair Revival). Carol Channing. *New York Daily News* 1981.

Pearl Bailey in *Hello, Dolly!* *Boston Globe* 1970.

One Flew Over the Cuckoo's Nest. Foreground: Kirk Douglas, Joan Tetzel. The others, l. to r.: William Daniels, Al Nesor, William Gleason, Malcolm Atterbury, Ed Ames. *New York Daily News* 1963.

110 in the Shade. Robert Horton wields the divining rod. The others, l. to r.:
Inga Swenson, Stephen Douglass, Will Geer, Steve Roland, Scooter Teague.
New York Daily News 1963.

I was telling my friend and classmate Joe Cooper of my curiosity about "stage plays," when his big sister, a senior at Jamaica Teacher's College, overheard us and suggested we attend Luther Davenport's Free Theater on East 28th Street in Manhattan. The term "Free" was important, because this was the depth of the Great Depression. I knew how to get there from Brooklyn because my weekly art classes had been nearby. It was Davenport and his company who first introduced me to the excitement of living theater. Between Acts Two and Three, Davenport appeared, draped in Roman toga, and appealed for

funds. When I had it to spare, I dropped a coin in the collection basket and thus enjoyed a few plays during my high school years. About fifteen years later, I happily revisited the theater, now known as the Gramercy Arts, to sketch a play called *The Honest-to-God Schnozzola*, featuring another former classmate, actor Salem Ludwig, and the debut of Herve Villechaise.

In the thirties I was unable to afford most Broadway attractions advertised in the newspapers, and was too young when the classic Civic Repertory Theater operated for ten years at low prices, until 1935. It was led by Eva LeGallienne, an eminent actress who believed that theater ideally should be as free as museums and libraries.

Eventually I was fortunate enough to see LeGallienne in a variety of plays. The first was a thriller called *Uncle Harry*, with that intriguing ham Joseph Schildkraut, in the early forties. Others were the rarely per-

formed Shakespeare *Henry VIII* and her own version of *Alice in Wonderland* (in which she played the Red Queen), both productions at the short-lived American Repertory Theater (1946–47). Later she appeared in several roles for Ellis Rabb's APA Repertory, including a notable Madame Arkadina in *The Sea Gull*.

Characteristic of her generation was a commitment to tour, and as a member of the National Repertory Company she played in productions of *The Crucible* and *The Madwoman of Chaillot*. I marveled at her great range and the thrilling energy, rarely encountered anymore, that she gave to big scenes.

Henry VIII. American Repertory Theater. Eva LeGallienne (Katherine), Victor Jory (Henry VIII).
New York Herald Tribune 1946.

142

The Royal Family. Revival. L. to r.: Eva LeGallienne, Mary Louise Wilson, Joseph Maher, Ellis Rabb, Sam Levene, Mary Layne, Rosemary Harris. *New York Daily News* 1976.

Exit the King. L. to r.: Patricia Conolly, Richard Easton, Eva LeGallienne. *New York Daily News* 1968.

Eva LeGallienne, National Repertory, left, in *The Trojan Women*; right, in *The Madwoman of Chaillot.*
Boston Globe 1965.

THE LITTLE SHOP OF HORRORS

There are many technical reasons why off-Broadway productions are not eligible for the Tony Awards, but artistic standards are not among them. A good example is the musical *The Little Shop of Horrors*, based on a fifties movie. The Drama Desk, which does not differentiate, conferred its award on *Little Shop* in 1983, while the Tony went to *Nine*. The latter ran for about a year on Broadway and *Little Shop of Horrors*, though playing in a small house on Second Avenue, lasted five and drew new investors like the Shubert Organization.

Little Shop of Horrors. Ellen Greene, victim of man-eating plant. Lee Wilkof to the rescue.
New York Daily News 1982.

FIRE

"You haven't made it until you've made it in New York" is the sentiment expressed in New York City's unofficial anthem. This testifies to the harsh and cynical reception awaiting those whose creative efforts are offered there for judgment.

A much different critical atmosphere pertains in cities with more normal quotas of cultural activity. When I resided for a few months in Dallas at the close of my army tour, my cultural editor at the *Dallas News* told me that the conductor of the Dallas Symphony, buoyed by the flattering reviews in the civic-minded local press, demanded a raise in his salary that was unwarranted by his name or national reputation. He was dismissed and replaced by Antal Dorati, who led the rejuvenated orchestra to a new level of recognition.

In 1968, an avant-garde play by John Roc, *Fire*, was presented by Brandeis University and enthusiastically received by the Boston press. Producer David Black decided to bring it to New York in early 1969. At a Drama Desk panel he detailed a budgetary structure and royalty plan based on an anticipated long run. An uneasy feeling came over me as he spoke, because there remained one minor hurdle for the Boston hit to clear: the New York critics.

To be sure, once again, an out-of-town smash was shot down and closed in a week. From what I saw, the judgment was severe. As Arthur Miller has since pointed out, there has been a healthy decentralization of theatrical activity taking place in recent years.

Fire. Foreground: Jennifer Darling and Rene Auberjonois. The others, l. to r.: Carolyn Coates, John Wardwell, Audra Lindley, Peter MacLean, Roy K. Stevens, Louis Edmonds.
New York Daily News 1969.

In June 1943, just before I left for army service, I was assigned to sketch the operetta *The Vagabond King* starring John Brownlee as the poet François Villon. In the caption, my venerable editor Arthur Folwell noted that the operetta was based on Justin Huntly McCarthy's play *If I Were King*, in which E. H. Sothern starred. This was my first encounter with the name Sothern and here he was, linked to my drawing! I looked him up and found that he was a great Shakespearean actor who made a tremendous hit in *If I Were King* in 1901. Just before his retirement, his Shakespearean company toured the United States extensively from 1919 until 1924, exposing thousands of Americans to the classical tradition.

Since my playgoing began in the early thirties and I did not recall seeing Sothern in a film, he was, up to that point, out of my frame of reference.

Which leads me to January 1980 when my newly appointed theater editor, the youthful Susan Toepfer, assigned me to do a large drawing of Rex Harrison and Richard Burton preparing to revive their greatest stage triumphs, *My Fair Lady* (1956) and *Camelot* (1960) respectively. She asked me to depict the aging stars as paunchy, jowly, wrinkled, and feeble. I quickly pointed out that "they may be good," and we would be unfair to put them down in advance. An impasse ensued and, as though summoned by a messenger, features editor Jack Sanders saun-tered by and Toepfer told the big boss what she had in mind.

"They may be good," said he, absolutely without my coaching. Toepfer backed down and the resulting drawing showed them polishing each other for their revivals.

In both cases the revivals were well received, although Rex Harrison's Henry Higgins had the ninety-year-old Cathleen Nesbitt playing his mother and Richard Burton, magnetic as ever, had to leave after a short time because of severe bursitis in his shoulder. He was succeeded by his friend Richard Harris for a long run and subsequent tours.

Rex Harrison and Richard Burton prepare to revive *My Fair Lady* and *Camelot*.
New York Daily News 1980.

Another Harrison triumph: *Emperor Henry IV*. L. to r.: David Hurst, Rex Harrison, Eileen Herlie.
New York Daily News 1973.

I will gladly give extra time, travel extra distances, and even incur expense in order to see in the flesh what I am assigned to draw. I can then circumvent the restrictions of what was photographed or left un-photographed.

The *Herald Tribune* sent me to sketch John Gielgud's production of *The Importance of Being Earnest* in Baltimore, where it was tuning up prior to Broadway. I arrived by train in time for a comfortable dinner next to the theater and settled in to sketch Wilde's delightful play. As the opening scene warmed the audience with Lady Bracknell's rib-tickling interrogation of John Worthing on his qualifications to win her daughter's hand in marriage, smoke seeped into the stage from the wings, implying something more intense than warmth. In seconds, the smoke from a fire in the restaurant next door became so thick that Gielgud had to inform the audience that the play could no longer continue. The theater was quickly vacated and I feared I'd have to resort to photos to meet my deadline.

I looked at my sketches of the opening scene, which I realized was as typical as any in the play. Twenty minutes in Baltimore gave me all I

The Importance of Being Earnest. L. to r.: Pamela Brown, John Gielgud, Margaret Rutherford. *New York Daily News* 1947.

Stephen Sondheim's successful 1970 musical, *Company*, has had well-received revivals in recent years, off-Broadway and in London. It has also been newly recorded. For me it will always be associated with a significant turning point in musical history which does not relate to *Company* itself. In "The Ladies Who Lunch" in Act Two, the bored and jaded urbanite played by Elaine Strich in the original cast sings cynically of the chic pastimes of her circle, referring at one point to "perhaps a piece of Mahler's—I'll drink to that!"

With that glancing reference an entirely new level was reached in the evaluation of Gustav Mahler. Who would have thought he would ever become *chic*. Those of us devoted to this formerly abused composer would have settled for his place alongside the other greats in the standard symphonic repertoire. And the single most effective force in achieving that status was Sondheim's friend and collaborator Leonard Bernstein, who, as music director of the New York Philharmonic at the height of his popularity, launched an unprecedented Mahler festival in 1960, performing and recording all of the master's major works.

The leading man of *Company*, an eligible bachelor was Dean Jones, who played with a circle of married friends. Jones was unhappy with his role during the tryouts. Director-producer Hal Prince agreed to replace him after the opening because there wasn't enough time to break in a replacement. That valiant person was Larry Kert, who had established himself in his debut as the lead in *West Side Story*. This was typical of Kert's career. In this case Jones received all the attention and reviews and recorded the cast album. Kert carried the long run. This gifted performer never had a successful vehicle for his talents apart from *West Side Story* and *Company*.

Company. Dean Jones (with cake). The couples, l. to r. clockwise: Barbara Barrie and Charles Kimbrough; George Coe and Teri Ralston; Merle Louise and John Cunningham; Elaine Stritch and Charles Braswell; Beth Howland and Steve Elmore. *New York Daily News* 1970.

BORIS ARONSON, SCENE DESIGNER

In *Cabaret*, instead of a show curtain Aronson hung a huge metallic mirror under the proscenium arch, angled to reflect the entire audience. The purpose was to remind us that we could have been part of the same history depicted in Berlin just before the Nazi takeover. Aronson in- formed director Hal Prince, face- tiously, that this mirror effect would work only if the show was a hit and there was a full house to reflect.

However, for me the most re- markable effect wrought by Aronson was in his stage design for Arthur Miller's *The Creation of the World and Other Business*, when the Lord, in his rage at Adam and Eve, ex- pelled them from the garden. The playing surfaces were stony slabs made of translucent acrylic, and lights flashed on from *below*, igniting their entire world to deafening claps of thunder.

The Creation of the World and Other Business. Pre-Broadway cast. Top: Hal Holbrook, Stephen Elliott. Below, l. to r.: Eve (unidentified), Barry Primus, Mark Lamos, Bob Dishy. © 1972 *The Washington Post.* Reprinted with permission.

JAMES EARL JONES

I find it especially gratifying when a play authored by a black playwright, dealing with the Black Experience, succeeds on Broadway. To be a black actor is to suffer an additional minority handicap: there are simply fewer outlets for your gifts. It is therefore vital that organizations such as The Negro Ensemble Company receive financial aid to help create more black theater.

James Earl Jones is simply one of the finest actors performing today.

In *Fences* his stature and magnetism made the most of his role as a former Negro League ballplayer, resentful of his son's easier success as an athlete.

Included here is his unforgettable role as the first black heavyweight champion in *The Great White Hope*, which also brought us Jane Alexander in her Broadway debut. Another success was his King Lear for the New York Shakespeare Festival, shown later on CBS-TV. His was the bass voice of the bemasked Darth Vader in the film *Star Wars* and he has appeared at least twice as Othello. The more recent version included the virtuosic Christopher Plummer as Iago, who created a considerable stir with his satirical approach to the role. Jones didn't enjoy becoming a straight man to Plummer's high jinks, especially when some laughs were coming at serious moments.

Fences. James Earl Jones.
Drama Desk News 1987.

King Lear. James Earl Jones, Tom Aldredge. *New York Daily News* 1973.

The Great White Hope. James Earl Jones, center, as Jack Johnson. Among the others, l. to r.: Jane Alexander, George Mathews, George Ebeling, Jimmy Pelham, Lou Gilbert. *New York Daily News* 1968.

Boesman and Lena. L. to r.: Zakes Mokae, Ruby Dee, James Earl Jones. *New York Daily News* 1960.

Othello. Dianne Wiest, above. Christopher Plummer, James Earl Jones. *New York Daily News* 1982.

Othello. L. to r.: Michael Higgins, Julienne Marie, James Earl Jones, Sada Thompson. *New York Daily News* 1964. (Jones's favorite production of *Othello.*)

Star Wars. Carrie Fisher, Mark Hamill. Above: David Prowse as Darth Vader (voice-over James Earl Jones).
New York Daily News 1979.

ALL YOU NEED IS ONE GOOD BREAK

A curious item in my collection is a drawing of a play called *All You Need Is One Good Break*; the drawing ran in the *New York Compass* in 1949. The play was the work of a new playwright named Joseph Paparofsky and dealt with a young man looking for shortcuts to success. In one of my rare departures from the journalistic axiom "protect yourself against dead news," my drawing appeared the Sunday after the opening, instead of before. Wouldn't you know it, bad reviews forced the play to close Saturday night. For Sunday, editor Sy Peck, having had no time to change the page, wrote the heading: "*All You Need Is One Good Break* got no break from the critics."

It is hard to say just how theater history would have fared had Paparofsky been a better writer or the critics kinder to his first play. In any case, he abbreviated his name to Papp, turned to directing in the new medium of television, then to producing free Shakespeare.

Eventually he expanded to include new plays such as Jason Miller's *That Championship Season*, David Rabe's *Sticks and Bones*, and the record-breaking Michael Bennett musical, *A Chorus Line*, to become *the* major producing force in the American theater.

All You Need Is One Good Break (by Joseph Paparovsky). L. to r.: Reuben Wendorff, Anna Appel, John Berry, J. Edward Bromberg, Lee Grant. *New York Compass* 1949.

Sticks and Bones. L. to r.: Cliff De Young, David Selby, Asa Kim, Elizabeth Wilson, Tom Aldredge.
New York Daily News 1971.

That Championship Season. L. to r.: Walter McGinn, Paul Sorvino, Richard A. Dysart, Michael McGuire, Charles Durning. *New York Daily News* 1972.

A Chorus Line. Top, l. to r.: Wayne Cilento, Priscilla Lopez, Pamela Blair. Below, l. to r.: Robert Lupone, Carole Bishop, Don Percassi, Renee Baughman. *New York Daily News* 1975.

GOOD

Recently, an important play by C. P. Taylor called *Good* was well received in an off-Broadway revival. The theme deals with a German professor of fine character who is gradually manipulated into the Nazi movement in 1933 and eventually finds himself an SS officer who will be sending thousands to their deaths.

The playwright used the varied music of the period, played by small combinations of onstage musicians to evoke the moods of the changing times, and I sketched the musicians in the background of my drawing. Dominating the scene was the professor donning his new SS uniform with the help of his wife.

My callow editor at the *News*, unfamiliar with the play, thought the musicians superfluous and despite my explanations, made me strike them. I found myself making a compromise akin to that of the professor in the play, but I did not want to appear insubordinate again, as in the Burton-Harrison affair, so I complied. Herewith my altered drawing for the original Broadway production.

Good. L. to r.: Michael Dansicker, David Howey (Hitler), Felicity Dean, Alan Howard. *New York Daily News* 1982.

169

TALLULAH IN
CRAZY OCTOBER

Tallulah Bankhead in
*Crazy October. Washington
Star* 1958.

The colorful publicist Richard Maney used to bemoan the fact that America's playwrights were unable to provide his most illustrious client, Tallulah Bankhead, with a vehicle worthy of her gifts. In the two decades that followed her triumph in *The Little Foxes*, she appeared in one flop after another.

I was spirited into a run-through of something called *Crazy October*. From the nonsense spoken before me, it was soon apparent that Tallulah's long wait for another hit was not over.

It must have been apparent to her as well, because at the finish, despite applause from the production family in the otherwise empty theater, Tallulah stood dejected, stage center. "What's wrong, Tallu, you were great!" called the director. "No, no, I was awful, just awful," and she wheeled right, pointing a finger at me in a side seat, J33, "and it's all his fault, sitting there, sketching."

I rose and approached her to point out that Maney had arranged for me to be there and create a six-column drawing for a newspaper in Washington, where she would open in a few days.

"Well!" she snarled with her deepest authority, "I hired Mr. Maney and I can fire Mr. Maney. You tell him he's fired!" and off she strode to her dressing room.

Now I had to sweat out the bad news that I'm the man who got Dick Maney canned! Next morning when I laid it on him, he smiled and asked, "Did you get your material? Do the drawing. Tallulah's fired me many times!"

The Milk Train Doesn't Stop Here Anymore. L. to r.: Ruth Ford, Tallulah Bankhead, Marian Seldes.
New York Daily News

I am the victim of a unique form of embarrassment when I find myself rocked with laughter at a rehearsal where everyone else present is thrice familiar with the material that's convulsing me. It's even worse when I'm moved to tears or a sob. I know that I'm proving the effectiveness of the play to the production staff, but that's no comfort to me.

Such was the case at a run-through of the very first *Odd Couple*, Neil Simon's durable comedy that has not ceased playing on stage, screen, and television; even in a sex-reversal revival on stage recently.

When the rehearsal was over and I was on my way out, director Mike Nichols asked me what I thought of the play (as though my guffaws hadn't already told him). In one word, "Hilarious!" I said, in spite of what I felt was a weak ending. I said nothing about that, because during the rehearsal period, playwrights try different endings. I assumed this would be improved later.

To be sure, Elliot Norton, dean of Boston critics, suggested that since the Pigeon sisters were so captivating, why not bring them back. This was done, for a fitting ending, by the author. Simon has spoken of a letdown after his plays open on Broadway. His work is done.

Unlike most playwrights, Simon thrives on last-minute changes.

The Odd Couple. Pre-Broadway tour. L. to r.: Walter Matthau, Art Carney, Carole Shelley, Monica Evans. 1965.

Featured in a revival of Strindberg's *The Father* was a young Philadelphia girl named Grace Kelly, making her debut as the tormented sixteen-year-old daughter of feuding parents.

A Philadelphia newsman came to the New York rehearsal to do a feature story on Kelly, whose family was well known back home. He approached press agent Harvey Sabinson and asked him to honestly appraise her talent, because if Grace was going places he would expand his piece accordingly.

"I'll level with you, since you ask. The best thing that could happen to this girl is for her to quit the theater, get married, and raise a family!" Like many enlightened theater people, Harvey likes to cite such incidents as samplings of his wisdom.

The Father. L. to r.: Raymond Massey, Mary Morris, Grace Kelly, Mady Christians. *The New York Compass* 1950.

The Father. Frances Sternhagen, Kate Porwin, Ralph Waite. *New York Daily News* 1981.

Irene Papas

We all have our special acting favorites, those rare personalities we'll indulge in whatever they care to play. One such for me was Irene Papas, ever since her haunting dark beauty cast a spell over me in the 1965 film *Zorba the Greek*.

So I greeted with great anticipation the announcement that she would appear on Broadway in Frank Gilroy's play *That Summer, That Fall*, in a role in which she was obsessively attracted to her stepson. Please note the two youngsters in the drawing: Jon Voight and Tyne Daly, newcomers in 1967. I was in awe of Papas at the rehearsal I sketched, though the play eventually failed. She then appeared impressively in a series of Greek classics; *Iphigenia in Aulis*, *Medea*, and *The Bacchae*.

The performances were on a thrust stage, sprawling before me in my second-row seat. Entranced, I found my attention focused on Papas throughout, even observing her *reactions* to the other players, out of range, situated elsewhere on the stage.

Medea. Irene Papas, center, John P. Ryan, at left. *New York Daily News* 1973.

That Summer, That Fall. L. to r.: Richard Castellanos, Irene Papas, Jon Voight, Tyne Daly.
New York Daily News 1967.

EQUUS

I never quite went along with the premise of Peter Shaffer's *Equus*—that the disturbed stable boy who gouged out the eyes of horses that had witnessed his love scene with his girlfriend was experiencing passion on a level unapproached by normal folk. What I did experience, however, was unique in its own way.

For several years I had admired the work of the beautiful and gifted actress Roberta Maxwell. I made it a point to see whatever she performed in.

So *Equus* was for me almost too rich an evening, when to my surprise she disrobed in her love scene with the boy!

Othello. Roberta Maxwell, thrown to the ground. The others, l. to r.: Jan Miner, Moses Gunn, Lee Richardson.
New York Daily News 1970.

Equus. Peter Firth, on horse (Everette McGill). The others, clockwise from bottom: Anthony Hopkins, Michael Higgins, Frances Sternhagen, Marion Seldes, Roberta Maxwell. *New York Daily News* 1975.

Romeo and Juliet. American Shakespeare Festival, Stratford, CT. David Birney, Roberta Maxwell.
New York Daily News 1974.

Everybody knows that Sherlock Holmes was really Basil Rathbone. That great actor played many other roles in films and luckily we were also able to see him live in the theater, too, as in *The Heiress* and in a special production of *Julius Caesar*, played in the round. We take thrust stages and theater in the round for granted today. In fact, many new theaters are now conceived in that form. In 1950, however, it was a novelty, and though it brings the entire audience closer than ever to the action, it creates other problems: You see the audience beyond the players (see my drawing), and you may miss facial expressions or words if the actor faces the other way.

Kevin Kline, rehearsing *Loose Ends* at Circle in the Square, irritated at having to keep turning, shouted to director Alan Schneider, "Who the hell invented theater in the round?" Schneider shot back, "The Marquis de Sade!"

Julius Caesar. Arena in the Hotel Edison. L. to r.: Emily Lawrence (Portia), Joseph Holland (Brutus), Basil Rathbone (Cassius), Sarah Burton (Calpurnia), Horace Braham (Caesar). *New York Compass* 1950.

Choreographer George Balanchine declined an invitation for the New York City Ballet to perform in a new Central Park Theater in the Round on the grounds that ballet was conceived to be viewed from one direction.

And where but for a proscenium stage could farceur Joe Orton have written the line in *Loot*, "This information must not go beyond these three walls!"

Getting back to Rathbone: in his later years he put together a program of Shakespeare readings with which he toured. In one instance he was booked to recite them as part of a concert in New York's Lewisohn Stadium, with a capacity of twenty thousand seats, where the New York Philharmonic played during the summer. That performance attracted three thousand patrons; more than Rathbone ever played to, but the smallest crowd to attend a Stadium Concert!

Basil Rathbone reading Shakespeare at Lewisohn Stadium, NYC, with the New York Philharmonic. *New York Daily News* 1963.

Basil Rathbone as Sherlock Holmes
(for use in a pipe ad).

NORKIN

J. B. Above: Frederic Worlock. Below, l. to r.: Michael Higgins, Eulalie Noble, Basil Rathbone (who also played part of the Broadway run). National tour, 1959–1960.

The Heiress. L. to r.: Edna Best, John Dall, Margaret Phillips, Basil Rathbone. Revived at the New York City Center. *New York Herald Tribune* 1949.

HAL HOLBROOK AS MARK TWAIN

Young Hal Holbrook, unemployed actor, selling hats in Macy's while waiting for a lucky break, came up with an interesting idea: he'd get his own act together by impersonating the elderly Mark Twain as he toured the lecture circuit, reciting from his works. Holbrook performed his program in a Greenwich Village nightclub in the mid-fifties without having to give up his job in Macy's, or later on, his acting in daytime television.

By 1959 he had developed two hours of material and opened in the off-Broadway Wurlitzer Theater on 42nd Street. It proved to be the sleeper of the season. When the editor of the *Daily News* read the raves in the other papers, he called

his off-Broadway critic, Charles McHarry, on the carpet to explain why he didn't even cover it! McHarry, ever respectful of the theater and particularly his off-Broadway domain, explained that Holbrook's *Mark Twain Tonight* was known to be a nightclub act and out of McHarry's jurisdiction. This was quickly corrected. As for me, I decided to attend with my sketch pad.

It did indeed turn out to be a memorable evening in the theater. Holbrook's makeup, which took almost two hours to apply, was remarkably convincing. Add to this his old, gravelly voice, and eyes that had seen a surfeit of suffering. After a while I had to stop sketching because, like a child, I became spellbound by his tales, delivered in the unhurried manner of the elderly but punctuated and underscored with a well-judged exclamation or gesture.

Then a phenomenal thing occurred. Mark Twain was nearing the end of his program. He paused as the smoke curled upward from his cigar, looked straight at the audience, and thanked them for coming and for being so attentive. I had become so taken with this wonderful, celebrated old gentleman that it saddened me to think I might never see him again!

I guess that is what theater can do at its very best, but I thought I had

gone to too many plays for it to happen to me.

Soon after my drawing appeared, Holbrook called me to acquire the original for his promotional use. I told him of my reaction to his performance and he was moved by it. The logo art has gone with him in ads, posters, and programs ever since. Mark Twain became the stepping-stone to a full career as an actor on stage and screen.

Incidentally, several years after using my logo he phoned to ask what I thought of a poster illustration of Mark Twain preparing to blow up the world (something the aging cynic had come to wish). I advised against it. Too negative to attract audiences.

Hal Holbrook portrays Twain, the lecturer, at seventy, telling how to quit smoking and about the life in the Sandwich Islands, Huckleberry Finn, a ghost story, and a drunk, in "The Shooting of Boggs." *New York Daily News* 1959.

FRIENDS

I sketched theater for the prestigious *New York Herald Tribune* for over a decade and appeared in newspapers across the United States, especially in theater tryout cities. The New York *Daily News* had a Sunday circulation of five and a half million, largest in the United States when my drawings first appeared there weekly, in an affiliation lasting over twenty-six years.

I am frequently asked whether I do anything similar to including the name "Nina" in my drawings in the manner associated with that senior practitioner at the *Times*. Two thoughts come to mind: Suppose his daughter was named Roberta, Elizabeth, or Stacy? Would it be equally facile to camouflage it within his linework? And shouldn't his inherent skill as caricaturist and designer be things he is known for? No. It's "Nina"!

There *is* something I've done that's special with me. My high school featured a dramatics society of extraordinary accomplishment under the tutelage of Dr. Elizabeth Cusack, a charter member of the Theater Guild. I enjoyed some minor triumphs in the leads of two plays, but two of my schoolmates were far more illustrious and made acting their careers. It didn't take too many years before our paths crossed, with my newspaper assignments taking me to their plays. I determined to work them into my drawings, no matter how small their parts.

As you can see from the 1942 *Miracle in the Mountains*, my friend Salem Ludwig is included although he uttered scarcely a line or two in his role as a monk. The bit parts continued and one afternoon I encountered him backstage at Ibsen's *An Enemy of the People* (the Frederic March production). "This time, Sam, it's going to be difficult because I appear in only one scene, the town meeting, which includes the entire cast!" Sketch it I did, and look for him in the full cast drawing, wearing the black bowler. I even named him in the caption and had to identify the rest of the players to do it, but the editor cut their names to save space.

Salem's extraordinary talent and sensitivity were recognized eventually, and his character parts grew larger, in *Wedding in Japan*, *The Hon-*est-to-God Schnozzola, *Awake and Sing*, Arthur Miller's *The American Clock*, and many other plays. Salem is an instructor at the renowned Actors' Studio.

Joseph Wiseman, another schoolmate, proved the easier assignment because he caught the attention of Katherine Cornell and became her protégé toward the end of her career. He is seen here in *That Lady* and has had an active career in serious theater but fame was thrust upon him in the form of an early James Bond film when he played the title role in *Dr. No*. His performing manner is stylized and arresting. Versatile, he gives a good account of himself in plays or films, from Shakespeare to T. S. Eliot, but on meeting him some time ago I inquired as to what was in the offing and he said, "I don't know. I'll take anything. Anything!"

An Enemy of the People. Frederic March, the speaker. Florence Eldridge, left. Morris Carnovsky, right. Salem Ludwig, in bowler at right. *New York Compass* 1950.

Miracle in the Mountains. Foreground: Victor Kilian, Julie Haydon, Frederic Tozere; above him: E. A. Krumschmidt; to the left of him: Monk Salem Ludwig. *New York Herald Tribune* 1947.

The American Clock. L. to r.: William Atherton, John Randolph, Salem Ludwig, Joan Copeland.
New York Daily News 1981.

That Lady. L. to r.: Henry Daniell, Henry Stephenson, Katherine Cornell, Torin Thatcher, Joseph Wiseman.
New York Compass 1949.

Murder in the Cathedral. Joseph Wiseman, center, attacked by Patrick Hines, Paul Sparer, Douglas Watson.
New York Daily News 1966.

Another venture into production occurred when I was asked by author-director Abe Burrows to create humorous sculpture for his musical *Can-Can* with a score by Cole Porter. He sought me as an artist because of my theatrical awareness, and was happily surprised when informed I *was* a painter and sculptor. He had expected only sketches from which a commercial sculptor would work. I eventually provided the maquettes (miniature sculptures) from which the enlargements were created under my supervision.

The story line involved a Parisian art critic whose rival for the love of a can-can dancer is a sculptor. The critic has occasion to review the sculptor's latest pieces. My assignment was to get laughs out of the sculpture without making them inept. I came up with a dozen ideas and Burrows selected three. The balance are still in his files. He used my titles and explanations in the dialogue. The three sculptures were designed to be combined as one in a final surprise gag.

A couple of the critics singled out that brief scene as being very funny, so Burrows's early warning to me that the whole idea might be struck if it didn't "work" was overcome. *Can-Can* enjoyed a long run.

Abe Burrows, directing. 1953.

Hans Conreid to Erik Rhodes: "The spirit of art rising from the Sea of Adversity. The fish must drown." 1953.

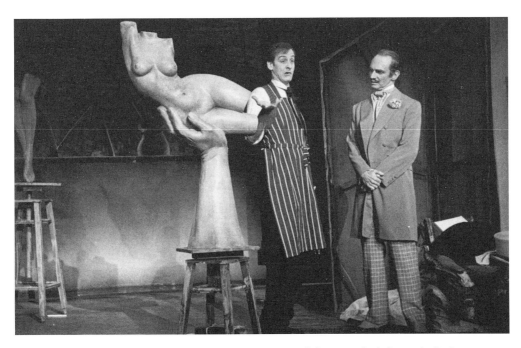

"The hand of the earth, yielding art treasures of the past. At left, symbolic legs. Spirit of the dance. Saves marble."

"Put them all together and you have the Maidmer; a less frustrating creature than the mermaid."

POPOV'S CLOWN ACT

During the first thaw in the Cold War in the fifties, *Porgy and Bess* and the Philadelphia Orchestra toured the Soviet Union, while the Bolshoi Ballet and the Moscow Circus came to the U.S. We all love our Ringling three-ring circus, but the Moscow Circus plays in one ring only and lets you concentrate on its clown acts, in the manner of America's smaller circuses that tour the countryside, or as in vaudeville years ago. The love and attention given to clowns has been one reason for the success of Cirque du Soleil and The Big Apple Circus. Recently David Shiner and Bill Irwin, two leading funnymen of varied acting and circus experience, teamed to do *Fool Moon*, a clown show, on Broadway.

But back then the legendary Popov was a star attraction in Russia, whereas the American circus played up the daredevil shot from a cannon. In his New York performance Popov walked the slack wire while twirling hoops on every limb or engaging in complex juggling.

Popov juggles at the Moscow Circus. USSR 1973.

While on a one-month tour of the Soviet Union in 1973, I attended the Moscow Circus and saw several additional Popov routines. In one he satirized Soviet medicine, impersonating a bumbling doctor who treats a drowned patient by stepping on his huge belly to release a spout of water from his mouth. What's so funny about that? He does it repeatedly with more water where that came from. The crowd roars.

In his next act, a U.S. Wall Streeter slinks in and places a huge A-bomb on a weight scale. Popov scampers in and removes his cap, revealing a live dove of peace on his head. He places the dove on the opposite tray of the scale and lo! Peace outweighs War. Applause!

My Popov sketches, made at that performance, are reproduced here for the first time.

Another first is to be found in the sad case of Nickel and Freckle, a Russian team that was the hit of the Big Apple Circus in 1978. My sketch of one of their delightful routines is seen here for the first time, because, much as the clowns were looking forward to it in the Sunday *News*, it never appeared, due to a prolonged newspaper strike and I haven't heard of them since.

Popov satirizes Soviet Medicine at the Moscow Circus. USSR 1973.

Popov sketch: *Peace Outweighs War.* Moscow Circus. USSR 1973.

Big Apple Circus. Nina Krasavina and Gregory Fedin as Nickel and Freckle. For *New York Daily News* 1978.
(Not published because of newspaper strike.)

David Shiner (top) and Bill Irwin in *Fool Moon. Stages* 1993.

Dreamy the Hippo (Ringling Circus). *New York Daily News* 1959.

During the several years that I contributed articles and reviews on the arts for the *Daily News*, the sports writer who used to pinch-hit as Yiddish theater critic left the paper for an editorship elsewhere, and because I knew the language, the territory was now mine. In this capacity I reviewed several Yiddish productions until the *News* enlarged its entertainment staff and I was no longer needed to help out.

One of its leading producers complained to me that the Yiddish theater was now being neglected by the *News* although the Puerto Rican and Black theater groups continued to receive coverage.

I suggested the producer take his case to the editor, who might not have been aware of the slight. This he did, probably with a degree of passion, because the next thing I knew, I was assigned, for the first time on the *News*, to sketch a Yiddish production, playing weekends in a high school auditorium. The drawing accompanied a long article by a free-lance writer on the current problems of the Yiddish theater.

Once Upon a Time. L. to r.: Ben Bonus, Elias Patron (as Sholom Aleichem), Reizl Bozyk.
New York Daily News 1977.

It has been rewarding to know the language. I was sketching a new Metropolitan Opera production, designed by Zeffirelli, of the two one-acters, *Cavalleria Rusticana* and *Pagliacci*, known as *Cav* and *Pag*. First I sat in on a studio rehearsal of *Cav* while Leonard Bernstein was directing leading tenor Franco Corelli in his concept of the role. During a pause he turned to me and Anne Gordon, press agent of the Met, to say, "He's not bad at all!"

When the session was over, we followed Bernstein down to the stage level where Fausto Cleva was leading an orchestral rehearsal of *Pag*. During a break, another great tenor, Richard Tucker, singing the lead, greeted Bernstein. I was waiting patiently to ask Tucker about his costume and was close enough to hear Tucker, the former Cantor, say in Yiddish, to Bernstein, composer of several Judaic works, "*Ich hub zu dir a—*") ("I have to you a—"), and he paused, groping for that special Yiddish word meaning "grievance." The word was *tynah* and I supplied it. Tucker looked at me with pleasure, finished his sentence, and continued in English. "You know I loved doing that Met Guild benefit yesterday afternoon when you asked me. But I had to do a performance in the evening which you didn't know about. I forgive you this time!"

Cav and *Pag* at the Met. Top: Leonard Bernstein. Center, l. to r.: Franco Corelli, Grace Bumbry, Franco Zeffirelli. Below: Fausto Cleva, Richard Tucker, Teresa Stratas. *New York Daily News* 1970.

The early decades of this century found the Yiddish stage in full flower and it spawned a number of eminent actors. With the passage of time, the Jewish-speaking population assimilated and the Yiddish theater audience dwindled, forcing many of the Yiddish actors to look to Broadway for work. Some even felt their expressive world was being plagiarized into English and aimed at the Jewish audience that no longer spoke Yiddish. In a desperate speech at the Drama Desk in 1975, decrying this trend, Herman Yablokoff, President of the Hebrew Actors' Union, proclaimed, "Look at *Fiddler on the Roof*. It's a Jewish play!" (The fact that this musical appealed to a vast audience across this country and abroad proved how universal its theme be.)

Joseph Buloff was a case in point. After an intense background in Yiddish theater, he scored a big success as the Persian peddler Ali Hakim in the original cast of *Oklahoma!* This brought him numerous other roles on Broadway. For me, his virtuosity was at its peak in *A Chekhov Sketchbook*, three one-act plays that were done off-Broadway. I also enjoyed his account, told with his Russian accent, of the troubles *Oklahoma!* ran into during the Boston tryout, with its legendary transition from out-of-town flop to Broadway hit. "Then they changed the name from *Let's Go Avay!* to *Oklahoma!*, and that did it!" (The show's original title was *Away We Go!*)

Fiddler on the Roof. Topol as Tevya. *Stages* 1990.

Joseph Buloff in *A Chekhov Sketchbook*. Top to bottom, he's seen as a prisoner in *The Vagrant*, an aged sexton in *The Witch*, and as a customer in *The Music Shop*. Helen Warren is the bellringer and Frank C. Borgman is the music dealer. *New York Daily News* 1962.

The Wall. L. to r.: George C. Scott, Leila Martin, Yvonne Mitchell, Joseph Buloff. Above them: James Ray, Al Verb. The Nazi is Robert Burr (with hound).

In 1969 I was invited to give a retrospective exhibition of my originals at the Lincoln Center Museum of the Performing Arts. I prepared some one hundred of my favorites and the show opened in August, scheduled to run into November. It proved popular enough to be held over into January 1970. Shortly afterward I had a follow-up engagement for several weeks in the Wright-Hepburn-Webster Gallery, which specialized in theater art, on 60th Street and Third Avenue. Both showings were accompanied by promotion and publicity, during which I was invited to write about my work, with illustrations, for the Carnegie Hall House Program. Julius Bloom, operator of Carnegie Hall, liked what I wrote and asked whether I would care to

review art for the program on a monthly basis. After some thought I found the offer irresistible and for two seasons I covered the important art shows for Carnegie Hall's concertgoers.

Meanwhile, at the *Daily News*, my colleague from the drama staff Lee Silver had become drama editor and had asked me to do pinch-hit reviews for the department when we were shorthanded. During the next few years I filled in on theater, ballet, opera, recitals, and symphony, but I was proudest of all to have initiated art reviews for the *Daily News*. Previously there had been no attempts at evaluation, only factual reportage.

Silver left the *News* for an executive position in the Shubert Organization (where he continues to make a valuable contribution in the area of expanding theater audiences) and Jack Sanders became my editor at the *News*.

Sanders decided to feature a year's-end section of critics' choices in the performing arts. I thought he would assign me to illustrate the feature. "No," he said, "I think I'd like you to make your own choices of the best you've seen, and illustrate *them*." Thus came into being what he named "The Norkin Awards— 1977," with the caption: "It would be difficult to find any individual who sees more of the performing arts in New York City than *Daily News* il-

lustrator Sam Norkin. These are his choices for the best in their categories over the past year."

The following year Sanders's wry heading for my panel read: "The Second Annual Norkin Awards." It also included a caricature of me by our staff artist, Bruce Stark, who sketched all the critics. I had submitted my self-caricature, along with photos, for his reference. He told me that in the interest of speed, he paraphrased my own caricature.

Then Jack Sanders retired and was replaced by his editorial assistant, Susan Toepfer, our rock and pop music authority.

At this point the cultural emphasis of the Sunday *News* entertainment section changed and the annual Norkin Awards were discontinued.

The Norkin Awards—1977

"It would be difficult to find any individual who sees more of the performing arts in New York City than *Daily News* illustrator Sam Norkin. These are his choices for the best in their categories over the past year."—Features editor, Jack Sanders.
New York Daily News 1977.

The Second Annual Norkin Awards.

THE NORKIN IMPERATIVE

I marvel at the contrast in the treatment of good news versus bad in the arts. A new venture is so orchestrated by the promotional forces that you cannot escape its birth. All media converge on you. But when a project dies, it is apt to disappear in silence and be mourned only by those few persons close to it.

So it was when the New York City Center quietly abandoned its musical revivals in 1968, and when the Lincoln Center Music Theater ceased to exist in 1969.

The former had operated for years, led by the resourceful Jean Dalrymple, who presented two seasons annually of several musicals each, drawn from the nation's qualified personnel, with whom she was keenly familiar, using sets and costumes she had acquired at the end of their Broadway runs.

Richard Rodgers, that superstar of composers, had undertaken as a labor of love the Lincoln Center project and for several years presented his revivals "with grandeur." When both venues ceased operation, I found the quiet deafening, so I began to investigate. I really missed the chance to rediscover *Pal Joey* or *Wonderful Town*. I had grown accustomed to seeing once again the great and less great American musicals. Drama critic Doug Watt, mindful of my emotional involvement in this pursuit, dubbed it "the Norkin Imperative."

In the case of Jean Dalrymple's musicals, they had been shot down by Clive Barnes, new drama critic of the *New York Times*. Barnes commented on a Christmas revival of *Carnival* in 1968, that the City Center ought to be devoting itself to nobler projects than the revival of routine musicals. (*Carnival* was originally a Broadway hit.) All the carefully acquired Dalrymple sets were then burned by a new City Center regime to save storage costs.

Frank Loesser rehearsing revivals of four of his musicals at New York City Center. *New York Daily News* 1966.

Richard Rodgers informed me that his last revival, *Oklahoma!*, had tried for a full summer's run (instead of one month for each of two musicals) and was unable to attract enough of an audience. So the Lincoln Center board abruptly terminated its Music Theater.

The question of subsidy arose. Opera was operating at a loss but musicals, because of their commercial potential, did not warrant institutional support.

I pointed out that the Vienna Volksoper, state supported, presented four American musicals in their repertory (*Kiss Me Kate*, *Show Boat*, *West Side Story*, and *Porgy and Bess*) but American foundations did not support their native product.

The issue of artistic merit arose. I interviewed authorities with the broadest of appreciations and drew emphatic affirmation of the value of the American musical. (In one instance I conferred with Betty Comden and Adolph Green, longtime collaborators on musical lyrics and books. I stumbled on a phenomenon heretofore never encountered: here were two persons thinking and speaking as one. He would start a sentence and she would finish it. The entire interview went that way, with the added word or phrase smoothly integrated in the concept.)

After numerous inquiries and the gathering of information, I contacted Anthony Bliss, general manager of the Metropolitan Opera, with my idea: when the regular season ends, have a summer season of operetta and musicals. The Met repertory already included *Die Fledermaus*, *La Perichole* and *The Gypsy Baron*. Add to this a few musicals and the revenue produced by them would help sustain the deficit-ridden operas. The orchestra could be split in two, with each production touring after its New York run. My bubble was quickly punctured. Bliss informed me that a warehouse fire had burned the sets and costumes of the operettas.

Although I hadn't touted my idea to the New York City Opera, Beverly Sills, its director, seems to have felt exactly as I did, because she made it happen. For several years the City Opera presented *Brigadoon*, *Candide*, *South Pacific*, *Sweeney Todd*, *Pajama Game*, *The Music Man*, and a number of operettas as standard fare.

Meanwhile, filling the void commercially, a whole slew of musical revivals surfaced, some of which stayed for long runs and tours.

As Doug Watt remarked, "We ought to be able to see the American musicals as often as an opera lover can enjoy *La Bohème*."

When the popular soprano Beverly Sills retired with honor from performing, she took over as impresario of the New York City Opera and was determined to enlarge its audience by broadening its appeal. She initiated supertitles above the stage to help overcome language barriers and expanded the repertory to include more operetta and Broadway musicals. The latter idea was opposed by some and caused the resignation of City Opera's longtime promotional head, Sheila Porter, who felt it was beneath the purpose of the opera to do so.

However, opera donor Lawrence Wein liked the idea and offered five million dollars to present five musical revivals in the five years to follow.

Now a curious new set of economic factors came into play, which changed completely the profitable production procedures of the Jean Dalrymple days at New York City Center twenty years earlier. New sets and costumes had to be manufactured instead of those salvaged from their Broadway runs, for example.

Guys and Dolls (revival). Nathan Lane and Faith Prince. *Stages* 1993.

In the ensuing years, several successful remountings of some better-known musicals, at top prices, set truly high standards, such as the 1990 revival of *Gypsy* with television's Tyne Daly and an earlier one with Angela Lansbury. Yul Brynner and Richard Kiley broke house records in their original roles reviving *The King and I* and *Man of La Mancha* respectively. Also successful were bright new mountings of *Anything Goes* and *Guys and Dolls*.

By comparison the five musical revivals by the New York City Opera, aside from the production of *The Pajama Game*, were unenthusiastically received. Some, like myself, were happy for the rare opportunity to see the original concept of *The Sound of Music* in a well-sung staging.

As the series ended, Sills had stepped down from her post in command to be succeeded by Christopher Keene, whose interest in Broadway musicals was somewhat cooler. The supporting donor, Mr. Wein, was now deceased and all his funds dissipated in his idealistic effort to mount fine productions for a greater audience at popular prices.

The Most Happy Fella (revival). Giorgio Tozzi. *New York Daily News.*

As a final gesture for Wein's generous idea I attempted to persuade my colleagues on the Drama Desk Awards Committee to cite him posthumously for a special award. I found insufficient interest in my suggestion and was ultimately discouraged when I sensed, in a call to the New York City Opera, that the company itself was relieved that the series was finished.

"But you retain in your repertory musicals like Bernstein's *Candide*, Weill's *Street Scene*, Sondheim's *Sweeney Todd* and *A Little Night Music*," I reminded the opera representative.

"They are *operas*!" I was informed. With that principle in mind, City Opera subsequently revived respectable productions of *The Most Happy Fella* and *110 in the Shade*.

South Pacific (revival). *New York Daily Times* 1967.

Pal Joey (revival). Bob Fosse and Carol Bruce. *New York Daily News* 1961.

Gypsy (revival). L. to r.: Crista Moore, Tyne Daly, Jonathan Hadary. *Stages* 1993.

Carousel (revival). L. to r.: Eileen Christy, John Raitt, Edward Everett Horton. *New York Daily News* 1965.

THE NEDERLANDER THEATER

Item from "On Stage, and Off,"
New York Times, January 28, 1994:

"The Nederlanders, by the way, will probably fill the traditionally hard-to-book Nederlander Theater on West 41st Street with *The Life*, Cy Coleman's new musical. The theater's problem has always been the neighborhood, but *The Life*, which is about whores and pimps in Times Square, should be reasonably at home. In any case, it won't arrive until the fall."

Recently, television star Stacy Keach ended a brief run of his one-man play, *Solitary Confinement*, at the Nederlander. It was the latest failure of The Broadway Alliance, a trade association, in initiating a series of plays at popular prices in marginal theaters. Earlier, *Our Country's Good*, a British import, reopened the darkened theater.

Some of my younger colleagues commented on how depressing they found approaching a theater set in such gloomy surroundings. Clive Barnes called the location "lousy" and producers have delayed openings rather than accept the proffered Nederlander. True, the theater is the only illuminated structure on the dark street. The nearest stores with lights are around the corner on Seventh Avenue, and they peddle pornography. Prospects for improvement are not bright, because the plans for rebuilding 42nd Street and Times Square have been suspended indefinitely, due to the recession.

The reaction of my friends triggered a flashback, spanning many years during which a palling blanket of darkness gradually descended on a warmly glowing theater enclave to snuff it out.

In the early forties, the National Theater, as the Nederlander was then known, housed Lillian Hellman's *The Little Foxes* starring Tallulah Bankhead in her greatest hit. About fifty yards further west I'd arrive at my place of employment, the *New York Herald Tribune*, only serious rival to the *New York Times*, in a city that boasted nine newspapers. At night a series of large white globes lined the facade of the *Trib*, with its name on each one. The bright lights were necessary because the other side of the street consisted of the dark stage doors of the 42nd Street theaters, which had by then become movie houses. Next door to the National was The Show Bar, a favorite intermission haunt of theatergoers and critics for a quick drink at a time when theaters had no bars.

More intriguing was Bleeck's Bar and Restaurant, marked "Formerly Club" on its sign in parentheses. This referred to its prohibition days when it was a speakeasy. Dorothy Thompson, esteemed political columnist of the *Herald Tribune* once interpreted "Formerly" as a name instead of an adverb, referring to Bleeck's as "The Formerly Club."

Bleeck's was not on 41st Street at all, but directly behind the National Theater, on 40th Street, separated in the rear by an alley and a fence. One fine day a door was installed in the fence and privileged persons were

Tallulah Bankhead. In *Midgie Purvis* with William Redfield, right, and young Pia Zadora, top left.
New York Daily News.

given keys to facilitate service. Thus Tallulah could be assured of fresh old-fashioneds before she went on each evening and swift transport from her dressing room to a hot supper after the show. Bleeck's was also the hangout for the *Tribune* gang, from editor to critic—all entering from the *Trib*'s 40th Street side, just next door. When Bleeck's went underground to become a speakeasy during prohibition, publisher Ogden Reid warned the Republican administration in Washington that the *Herald Tribune*, a stalwart Republican newspaper, would go Democrat if Bleeck's was raided. It never was.

Half a block east, on 40th Street, was the stage door of the old Metropolitan Opera, whose staff and patrons were to be found at Bleeck's. Add to this the cream of the garment center surrounding the restaurant and you get a good idea of what a busy "in" place Bleeck's was.

Back on 41st Street, at the corner of Seventh Avenue, you found a soda fountain, open evenings for theatergoers thirsting for an egg cream. Turn north and you had the Stanley Theater, a spillover from the 42nd Street movie houses. The Stanley showed Soviet films, like Eisenstein's *Alexander Nevsky* and *Ivan the Terrible*.

Nearby were other legit theaters like the Empire at Broadway and 40th, where *Life With Father* ran for seven years, and the Mercury Theater on 41st Street, one block east of the National, where Orson Welles, John Houseman, and Marc Blitzstein made history in the late thirties.

At one point, flamboyant showman Billy Rose purchased the National and after extensive renovation, gave it his name. Among his improvements was a roofing over of the eastern alleyway to create more lobby and intermission space. All to no avail, because the area started going downhill as the Billy Rose was deserted by its neighbors. The *Herald Tribune*, in decline along with other newspapers for a number of reasons, folded and became just another office building. Ditto for the Empire and Mercury Theaters.

The old Met was torn down by its owners with indecent haste, in a panicky move to checkmate possible competition, when its new house opened in Lincoln Center. Now most of Bleeck's patrons were gone. For a number of years the *Herald Tribune* alumni met there at Christmastime in sentimental reunion, until their host said his own goodbyes and shut his doors. The Show Bar, next to the theater, is boarded up. There is no soda fountain on the corner of Seventh Avenue. The Stanley Theater around the corner was razed and has been a parking lot for many years.

Eventually the Billy Rose was acquired by the Nederlanders and renamed again. For a while it was used as a church, until the congregation moved to larger quarters at the Mark Hellinger.

When the Martin Beck was constructed west of Eighth Avenue, years ago, some Gotham pundits predicted nobody would cross Eighth Avenue to see a show. The current hit revival of *Guys and Dolls* is the latest to prove them wrong. One producer rashly stated that theater buffs would even go to Jersey for a hit. So what's so bad about 41st Street? All we need is another hit to keep the lights on.

NORKIN

No actor is better known in the United States than "J. R." of the popular television series *Dallas*, which ended its lengthy run in May 1991. He is, of course, Larry Hagman and it hasn't hurt his career to be born the son of Mary Martin, legendary star of *South Pacific* and Peter Pan and singer of the hit "My Heart Belongs to Daddy." In fact, things came full cycle when Mary Martin eventually found herself known to a new generation as J. R. Ewing's mother!

In 1980, one *Dallas* episode earned full-page headlines in the tabloids—"WHO SHOT J. R.?"—the mystery confronting millions of television buffs.

That was the point at which I had to think back on the contrast with his obscure years in the sixties when he was a novice, remembered as his mother's son, trying to make it on Broadway. He never did, despite a citation from *Theater World* for his performance in *God and Mrs. Murphy*. He was also seen in *The Nervous Set*, a musical populated with hippies, and S. J. Perelman's comedy *The Beauty Part*, starring Bert Lahr in his favorite role.

Larry Hagman as J.R.

The Beauty Part (Bert Lahr's favorite play). Above, l. to r.: Larry Hagman, Alice Ghostley, Charlotte Baes, Bert Lahr (in five roles), Marie Wallace (the witness). Below: girl and gorilla (unidentified). *Philadelphia Bulletin* 1962.

God and Kate Murphy. L. to r.: Faye Compton, Larry Hagman, Lois Nettleton. *Boston Globe* 1959.

Tani Seitz and Richard Hayes in *The Nervous Set*. Thomas Aldredge (cigarette dangling from lips) is a gone poet who sleeps in the bathtub; Larry Hagman (emerging from the blanket) is a beat novelist who sleeps on the floor; Del Close (expounding) is a writer of exposes who sleeps anywhere. Frowning on the scene is a bust of Sigmund Freud. *New York Daily News* 1959.

ROBERT PRESTON

No career is more influenced by the vagaries and vicissitudes of fate than that of the actor. It is most important he be in the right place at the right time. Take Robert Preston. He made scads of B movies that never exploited his potential. He turned to the stage.

In his maturity, along came *The Music Man*. This was a new Broadway musical which was turned down by a number of stars, including Danny Kaye. (Perhaps the character seemed too unsympathetic. Henry Fonda never forgave his agent for rejecting *Who's Afraid of Virginia Woolf.*)

His creation of the Music Man on stage and later on screen, became the yardstick by which his many successors in the role were measured. And he went on to a long series of worthy stage roles, including Henry II in *The Lion in Winter*. He returned to the screen, but this time in better roles, in important films.

The Music Man. Barbara Cook and Robert Preston. *New York Daily News* 1957.

We Take the Town. L. to r.: Mike Kellin, with knife; Robert Preston, with gun; Carmen Alvarez, with cigar; John Cullum aims camera; Romney Brent, writing; and Kathleen Widdoes, with fan. *Philadelphia Bulletin* 1962.

So, after all this, he gives an interview in which he is asked to reflect on his career and name his favorite role. Without flinching he says Pancho Villa in the musical *We Take the Town*. You never heard of it? Well, I sure did. I spent an afternoon sketching a run-through for the *Philadelphia Bulletin*. It was one of the many theatrical leviathans to sail away and fail to return for its scheduled Broadway opening. (For more examples, see next story.)

In a similar interview, the great and versatile Hume Cronyn, boasting a string of roles the envy of any actor, confided that *his* favorite role was in *The Man in the Dog Suit*, one of his least successful plays, but one in which the central character was transformed by his masquerade costume.

The Lion in Winter. Robert Preston, foreground. The others, l. to r.: James Rado, Dennis Cooney, Bruce Scott, Rosemary Harris, Anne Fielding. *Boston Globe* 1966.

The Man in the Dog Suit. Jessica Tandy and Hume Cronyn. *Washington Star* 1958.

THOSE SHOWS THAT NEVER CAME BACK

There was a time when it was absolutely de rigueur for a show to book a pre-Broadway out-of-town tryout tour. The reasons were sound: changes, cuts, experiments, and improvement of flow all take place before audiences and critics that allow for a work in progress, and away from a destination where hostile word-of-mouth can kill a production before it has a fair chance.

A basic change took place, however, after the remarkable success of *Who's Afraid of Virginia Woolf?* Albee's play was a hit with only a few weeks of New York previews in which to tune up. Many producers have been trying to save on pre-Broadway tours ever since.

But, because of my contributions to newspapers in tryout cities like Boston, Philadelphia, Washington, New Haven, Toronto, Montreal, Wilmington, Baltimore, Detroit, Cleveland, Pittsburgh, Chicago, Los Angeles, and San Francisco, I was privy to the incubation of most shows that did tour.

Alas, many failed to make it back to New York for the announced opening. In some cases, it was obvious to me at rehearsals that a time bomb was being shipped to an unsuspecting city as I waited for it to detonate. After some years, I realized that I had collected a goodly number of these mementos of failure by way of my drawings. In some cases, they are the only record of what the show looked like, because after the opening night reviews, with the future looking hopeless, the producer, not wishing to throw good money after bad, canceled the photo call (second night) to save a thousand dollars.

I include a representation of those shows for the curious and for the sake of theater buffs among my readers. There existed in the tryout cities a fanatical band of theater lovers, cognizant and appreciative of the historic portent of their location. They were in a position to witness the birth of a *My Fair Lady, South Pacific, Kiss Me Kate* or *Fiddler on the Roof.* They could attend the world premieres and compare notes with the likes of Elliot Norton or Richard Coe, then return a week or two later to make note of script or cast changes. They could catch the last night in town and even travel to the next tryout city, or follow the show to New York for its gala Broadway opening. One such "showfreak," as he calls himself, is my friend *TheaterWeek* columnist Peter Filichia. I find it great fun to pull clips from my files of the rarities he encounters in his pursuits, those "forgotten" shows that he remembers. Some have been reborn today, after failing to survive their original debuts during a time of overwhelming competition from big hits. As to those that never made it to New York, remember that top stars, authors, composers, and producers have withdrawn works headed for Broadway. It is to their credit that they felt the product unworthy of their reputations or their audiences. In other cases the shows were underfinanced, in need of too much revision for the schedule, or, oddly, had no theater available in New York to house them.

Royal Flush. L. to r.: Kenneth Nelson, Jill O'Hara, Mickey Deems, Kaye Ballard (statue actress unidentified). (No photo call.) *Toronto Star* 1964. *Philadelphia Bulletin* 1965.

Miss Moffat (Emlyn Williams, Joshua Logan, Albert Hague). L. to r.: Dody Goodman, Dorian Harewood, Marian Ramsey, Bette Davis, David Sabin, Avon Long. *Philadelphia Bulletin* 1974.

Juniper and the Pagans. L. to r.: Mario Alcade, Ellen Madison, David Wayne. *Boston Globe* 1959.

Prettybelle (Jule Styne, Bob Merrill, Gower Champion). L. to r.: Mark Dawson, Angela Lansbury, Peter Lombard, Jon Cypher. *Boston Globe* 1971.

The Gay Felons. L. to r.: Denise Darcel, Alan Ansara, Jacques François, Luba Lisa, Josef Elic, George Tobias. Wilmington, Delaware 1959.

The Ziegfield Follies. L. to r.: Carol Haney, David Burns, Tallulah Bankhead, Joan Diener, two dancers.
Boston Globe, Philadelphia Bulletin 1958.

The Hemingway Hero by A. E. Hotchner. L. to r.: Jennifer West, Gary Merrill, Norman Rose, Lois Nettleton. *Boston Globe* 1967.

Motel. Top: Vicki Cummings, Myron McCormick. Below: Siobhan McKenna,
Richard Easton. *Boston Globe* 1960.

One Foot in the Door. L. to r.: Barbara Kay, Frances Helm, Barbara Hall, June Havoc.
Philadelphia Bulletin 1957.

Prescription, Murder. L. to r.: Agnes Moorehead, Thomas Mitchell, Joseph Cotten, Patricia Medina.
Boston Globe 1962.

Enrico. L. to r.: Alida Valli, Charles Korvin, Burgess Meredith, Delphine Seyrig, Dario Barri.
Philadelphia Bulletin 1958.

Listen to the Mockingbird (Edward Chodorov). L. to r.: Eva Le Gallienne, Una Merkel, Billie Burke. (Closed after theater fire in Washington.) *Boston Globe* 1958.

A Sign of Affection. L. to r.: Leslie Ann Warren, John Payne, Nan Martin. Pre-Broadway Tour.
Philadelphia Bulletin 1965.

A Swim in the Sea. L. to r.: Inga Swenson, Fay Bainter, Robert Carraway, Jean Stapleton, Carol Stone.
Philadelphia Bulletin 1958.

Two Weeks Somewhere Else. L. to r.: Philip Bruns, Pat Englund, David Kosoff, Pat Englund (plays both women). *Boston Globe* 1967.

The Joker. L. to r.: Anne Kimbell, John Boyd, Marjorie Gateson, Tommy Noonan. *Philadelphia Bulletin* 1957.

Several years ago, *The Last Temptation of Christ*, a Martin Scorsese film, became a source of heated controversy. In France, some theaters showing it were burned out by offended fundamentalists.

Films centered on the life of Christ, it seems, have always stirred controversy. The only differences have been a matter of degree. For the Easter season of 1980, NBC television repeated a six-hour 1977 miniseries by Franco Zeffirelli called *Jesus of Nazareth*, with stars such as Laurence Olivier, Anthony Quinn, Anne Bancroft, and Rod Steiger. British actor Robert Powell starred as Jesus. Fundamentalist protests during the 1977 showing had been overcome only through acclaim by the television critics.

I was asked by my editor to paint a color portrait of Powell in the role for the cover of the *Daily News* television magazine, reducing the size of the crown of thorns and eliminating the streams of blood. The caption read simply: "Robert Powell in *Jesus of Nazareth*."

As usual, protests were received anyway. The prize was one from a lady who declared that the illustration didn't look like Jesus!

Jesus of Nazareth. Robert Powell. *New York Daily News* 1980.

Jesus Christ Superstar. Jeff Fenholt (Christ), Bob Bingham (above, center).
New York Daily News 1971.

I was hired by John Chapman, drama critic and drama editor of the *Daily News*, as weekly theatrical caricaturist and worked for him until his retirement fifteen years later. He was known to many as an old curmudgeon and even referred to himself as Old Frostface in his writings. He smiled only grudgingly, under a red bulbous nose that cradled his horn-rimmed glasses.

In spite of his tough exterior, he was a discerning critic, dedicated to his love of the theater and opera. He was also loyal to his staff. In one instance he came to my rescue when a publicist withdrew my press seats because I sketched a show other than his. Chapman informed the press agent that he was responsible for the assignments and he'd be happy to return his own opening night tickets if Norkin was not welcome. I was re-invited.

In his review of *Camelot* he complained of a "down" ending, pointing out that *The Once and Future King*, the source of the musical, held out hope for the future. In an unusual development, the authors did improve the last scene and, as we all know, *Camelot* enjoyed a long run and many revivals.

Later, after his review of *Fiddler on the Roof*, which he called one of the greatest musicals of the century, I asked why he didn't complain about the "down" ending of *Fiddler*, wherein the Russian Jews are sent packing from their hometown, Anatevka. "Hell, that's no down ending. They're headed for America!"

He suffered from gout. One evening, on alighting from his cab for an opening at the Playhouse Theater on 48th Street near Seventh Avenue, he found a parking garage where the theater should have been. Looking at his tickets, he discovered that the Playhouse Theater was now at a new 48th Street number near Ninth Avenue. With no taxi in sight, he proceeded to limp west and finally reached the new theater, a converted church where the orchestra is two flights above street level. After all this, the play turned out to be *Ghandi*, a one-man show starring Jack McGowran. It was a failure. Chapman left after one act, unusual for him, the evening a total washout.

He was enthusiastic over the new Shakespeare theater at Stratford, Connecticut, not far from his home in Westport, and covered its productions regularly. Making it a point to arrive at the theater early, he found himself seated at a new production of *Henry V* starring Len Cariou only to observe the stage filled with gymnasts in action. Reaching for an usher, he inquired as to whether this was some preliminary event, since he saw nobody on stage dressed for Shakespeare. Assured that yes, it was Shakespeare, he now asked which play was being given. Informed that it was indeed *Henry V* and "this is how it begins," he scowled, "The hell it does!" And with that, he rose, hobbled up the aisle and headed back to Westport with Mrs. Chapman.

The annual visit of the Ringling Circus was the subject of a drawing each time they came to New York. I would alternate a panel of new acts with a study of one of the animals. The drawing seen here shows one of the circus dancing girls seated atop an elephant's head. What was remarkable about it was the size on the page. Chapman gave it the big play.

Fiddler on the Roof (revival). L. to r.: Thelma Lee, Zero Mostel, Duane Bodin
(Grandma's Ghost). *New York Daily News* 1976.

When I asked why the special treatment, he said, 1) he liked the drawing, and 2) it was an inside tribute to Bill Fields, dean of theatrical press agents, currently promoting the circus, and seriously ill.

I agreed that Fields was a top-notch professional, but wasn't the dean of PR realy Dick Maney, who promoted *My Fair Lady* for a seven-year run?

"Dick Maney hasn't shown his ass in this office for ten years!" scowled Chapman. "Fields isn't too big for his job to pay us a visit."

It was customary for me to remind him of the upcoming theater calendar from which he would select my assignment. Early on, a dilemma arose. I informed him that a new Tennessee Williams play was opening the same week as the new Rodgers-Hammerstein musical. Which one? "Neither," he answered. "Do the opening of the Metropolitan Opera!" I don't think he realized he was talking to a music lover—opera buff, but it was the beginning of a series of many opera drawings.

In another instance I cited two more important openings taking place in the same week, wisecracking that the choice for the drawing was *his* problem. "That's easy," he said, "Do both!"

"Do both?" I whined. "Do you realize what you're asking?"

"Now, that's *your* problem." He had me there. I never tried to outwit him again.

Henry V (Strafford, CT). Len Cariou. *New York Daily News* 1969.

MINYAK

You may be convinced that if you've seen one elephant you've seen 'em all. If so, you would be doing an injustice to Minyak, the lead pachyderm of the Ringling Circus, who starred in Cecil B. DeMille's 1952 circus epic, *The Greatest Show on Earth*, in which he proved himself a true professional, able to take direction. In a suspenseful scene, he held his hoof inches over the head of a beautiful equestrienne sprawled on the ground.

He is equally at home in this 1961 drawing for the Ringling Circus, where he is crowned by Kelly Ann Holmes, a circus chorine.

I was flattered when Doug Wilson, art director of the *News* posted a full-size copy of the original over his table in the heart of the newsroom.

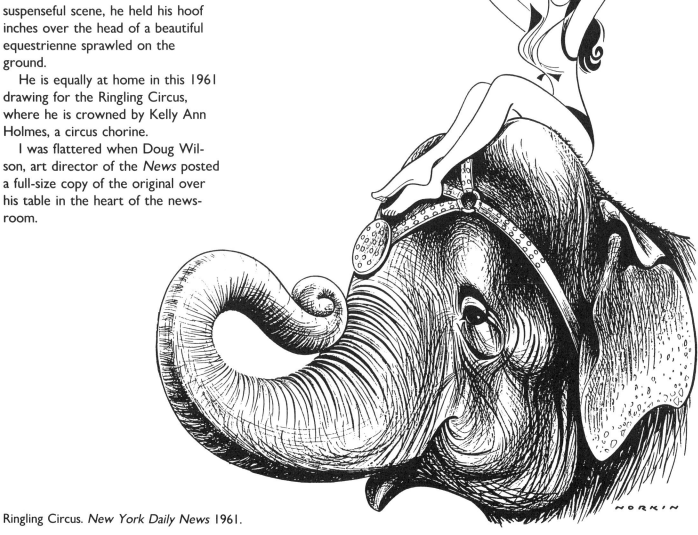

Ringling Circus. *New York Daily News* 1961.

253

THE MET

My drawings usually took note of the Met's openings, but more often, I sketched the new productions at their dress rehearsals. The Met borrowed the originals for an ongoing exhibition in its intermission guest room that lasted twenty years. Some are seen here, along with those of the New York City Opera.

Peter Grimes. Metropolitan Opera. Lucine Amara, Guy Curtis, Jon Vickers. *New York Daily News* 1967.

Pelleas and Melisande. New York City Opera. Louis Quilico (Golaud) discovers wife Patricia Brooks (Melisande) and Andre Jobin (Pelleas) in love scene at window. *New York Daily News* 1970.

The Sicilian Vespers. Metropolitan Opera. L. to r.: Justino Diaz, Montserrat Caballe, Nicolai Gedda, Sherrill Milnes.
New York Daily News 1974.

Otello. Metropolitan Opera. Sherrill Milnes (Iago) stands above James McCracken (in the title role). "Here Lies Your Lion!" *New York Daily News* 1972.

Mefistofele. New York City Opera (hit revival). Top: Carole Neblett as a vision seen by Robert Nagy, as Faust. Norman Treigle is Mefistofele, on pedestal. *New York Daily News* 1969.

Boris Godonov. Metropolitan Opera. Martti Talvela as Boris, Paul Offenkrantz, on throne. (Ming Cho Lee, scenery).
New York Daily News 1975.

Mourning Becomes Electra. Metropolitan Opera. L. to r.: Evelyn Lear, John Reardon, Marie Collier.
New York Daily News 1967.

Otello. Metropolitan Opera. Placido Domingo, Gilda Cruz-Romo. *New York Daily News* 1974.

Lucia Di Lammermoor. Metropolitan Opera. Joan Sutherland and Robert Merrill. *New York Daily News* 1964.

Fidelio. Metropolitan Opera. "First kill his wife!" L. to r.: Jon Vickers, Leonie Rysanek, Giorgio Tozzi, Walter Berry.
New York Daily News 1960.

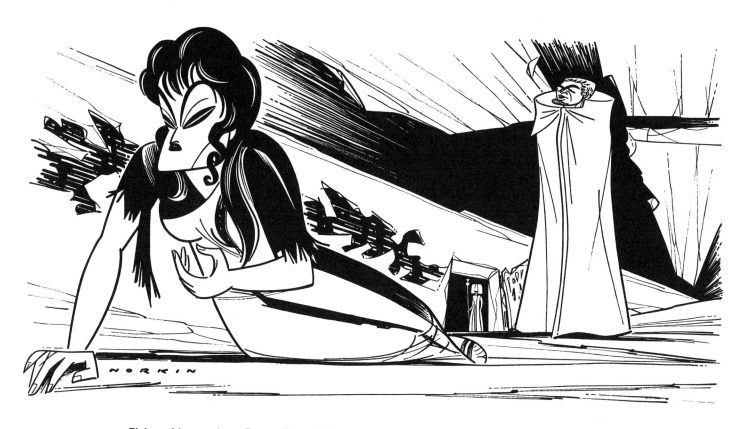

Elektra. Metropolitan Opera. Birgit Nilsson and William Dooley. *New York Daily News* 1966.

American operas at New York City Opera. Top, *The Scarf*: Richard Cross, Patricia Neway. Below, l. to r., *Wuthering Heights*: John Reardon, Phyllis Curtin. *The Devil and Daniel Webster*: Walter Cassel, Norman Kelley (with fiddle). *Street Scene*: Helena Scott, David Poleri. *New York Daily News* 1959.

NEW OPERATIC CONCEPTS

Opera, like other forms of theater, is not immune to new concepts. Quite the contrary. There is a smaller repertory of sure-fire hits in opera, so innovative approaches are apt to be more welcome.

At a dress rehearsal of Wagner's *Tristan und Isolde* in 1971 at the Met, some daring new ideas were invoked to enhance the love scenes between Birgit Nilsson and Jess Thomas in the title roles. After un-

wittingly drinking Brangaene's love potion they embraced illicitly in broad daylight on board the ship bearing Isolde home to wed King Mark.

Leinsdorf

Tristan und Isolde. L. to r.: Mignon Dunn, Birgit Nilsson, Jess Thomas. *New York Daily News* 1973.

Slowly the light faded and the lovers were enveloped in a whirl of color. Soft tones of turquoise and violet entwined them as, ever so gradually, they were magically raised some twenty feet above the deck by an invisible elevator. All the while they sang passionate declarations of their mutual love, fortified by an unleashed orchestra.

Remember, we were at a rehearsal where precious time was meant to be used to polish the performance. The conductor was apt to stop short and call his cue number in the score for instructions and a fresh start. Erich Leinsdorf was the maestro in this case and at the very moment described above, he rapped his baton on the stand, interrupted the music and shouted, "Sixty-nine! I want sixty-nine!"

The battle of directorial concepts will rage on, fueled by those on the one hand jaded by tradition and the others who place value on authenticity.

One of my favorite operas is Richard Strauss's *Salome*. I never miss a new production of it if possible. I first became familiar with *Salome* on the printed page in Oscar Wilde's poetic play version. When I learned that Strauss had used Wilde's text almost verbatim (in translation, of course) I couldn't wait to see and hear it.

The daring opera, a triumph of program scoring, was censored at the time of its premiere in 1906 and broke new ground in its depiction of sexuality and the outre. It drives inexorably to its bloody conclusion in its adherence to Wilde's structure.

I've been spellbound by some of the productions I've seen over forty years: in particular, with convincing Salomes like Phyllis Curtin, Maralin Niska, and Grace Bumbry. In 1992, the rarely seen Wilde play was presented by the Circle in the Square company, with Al Pacino as the befuddled sensualist Herod. His Salome shed all her veils during her dance, falling to her knees before him, quite nude, then sprawling backward. Critic John Simon wrote that Herod's slave, seated at his feet, enjoyed the best location in the house.

Recently I attended the new version at the Metropolitan Opera, reconceived by Nikolaus Lehnhauff, and was stunned by the utter disregard for the composer's intentions. Had it not been for the superb conducting by James Conlon and the glorious sounds from his orchestra, it would have warranted outright rebellion.

First we had an overweight Salome, Hildegarde Behrens. That's O.K. We can live with that, if the spirit is there, as in the case of Luba Welitch or Birgit Nilsson. But when all is at stake after extensive bargaining with Herod, she sheds her veils in a supposedly sensual dance to reveal herself, not implicitly nude, but as a klutz in a long nightgown. Had I been Herod, I would have jailed her on the spot for fraud!

In a previous scene, Jochanaan scorns her passionate pleas for a kiss and returns to his cistern. The music wells up to illustrate Salome's sexual frustration in quite graphic terms. Here, Behrens simply donned Jochanaan's abandoned shawl, in total disregard of what the composer called for.

Salome. Metropolitan Opera. Grace Bumbry performs her Afro-oriented dance over the cistern of John the Baptist for the pleasure of Robert Nagy (Herod) and Regina Resnick (Herodias). *New York Daily News.*

The opera is set on a terrace outside Herod's palace. There is no question of this, because much is made of the evolving moon. The lunar leitmotif is recurrent and changes as events shift during the opera—finally glowing to reveal Salome's ultimate aberration as she consummates her kiss on the lips of Jochanaan's severed head.

But where are we to find a moon in a scenic concept that places the entire opera *indoors*, in a tilted set that has an audience concerned for the safety of singers coping with its hazards? Yes, I heard Strauss's haunting moon music, but stripped of context. FInally, this "daring" new production, updated from biblical to modern times, chickened out when it came to Salome's execution. The curtain fell with the princess intact, thoroughly ignoring Herod's peremptory death sentence.

A conceptual fiasco! Altogether one of the most glaring cases of its sort. And at the Met.

Salome. New York City Opera. Maralin Niska, William Neill (Herod). *New York Daily News* 1975.

Salome. Metropolitan Opera. L. to r.: Birgit Nilsson, Irene Dalis, Karl Liebl. *New York Daily News* 1965.

LINCOLN CENTER WATCHING

THOUGHTS OF A TROUBLEMAKER ON THE OCCASION OF THE MET'S 25TH ANNIVERSARY AT LINCOLN CENTER

Sidewalk superintendents have enjoyed official recognition for some time now. Every fence surrounding an excavation respectfully acknowledges the curious with small windows or peepholes. When plans for Lincoln Center were announced during the Eisenhower years, I hung on every word to be found in the press and became a watcher when construction began. New York had never planned anything like it for culture!

Lincoln Center is an architectural triumph. It succeeded in integrating the designs of several major architects by their agreeing on common denominators of dimension and material but allowing for originality within those precepts. Its three basic structures form an embrace for all who enter its plaza. It has functioned well despite severe growing pains and major gaffes. Logistically, the predicted congestion never proved a major problem. Staggered starting times became unnecessary.

However, I would like to take note here of some of the bizarre facts regarding Lincoln Center.

The first oddity came about when the Metropolitan Opera, headed for Lincoln Center and shuddering at the thought of competition, sold its old home on the condition it be demolished forthwith. Howls of protest arose on the artistic grounds that its fine acoustics were a known quantity, while the new house under construction was a question mark. Conducting a farewell concert there one evening, Leopold Stokowski embarrassed his hosts by turning to the audience to urge that they save the old Met from the wrecker's ball. Commercially, impresario Sol Hurok also protested, pointing out that three-thousand-seat houses made grand productions feasible. He was quickly silenced by a generous deal for use of the new Met.

Up on 57th Street, Carnegie Hall was vacated by the New York Philharmonic when it moved to Lincoln Center, and sold to a developer who planned to raze it and erect a dandy new pink office building. Violinist Isaac Stern, in tune with public sentiment, organized a foundation that saved the house that Peter Ilich Tchaikovsky inaugurated in 1891 and that gained world renown for its superb acoustics.

Philharmonic Hall (later renamed Avery Fisher Hall, in honor of the hi-fi tycoon who financed a second major reconstruction to correct flawed acoustics) was the first structure to be completed at Lincoln Center, in 1962.

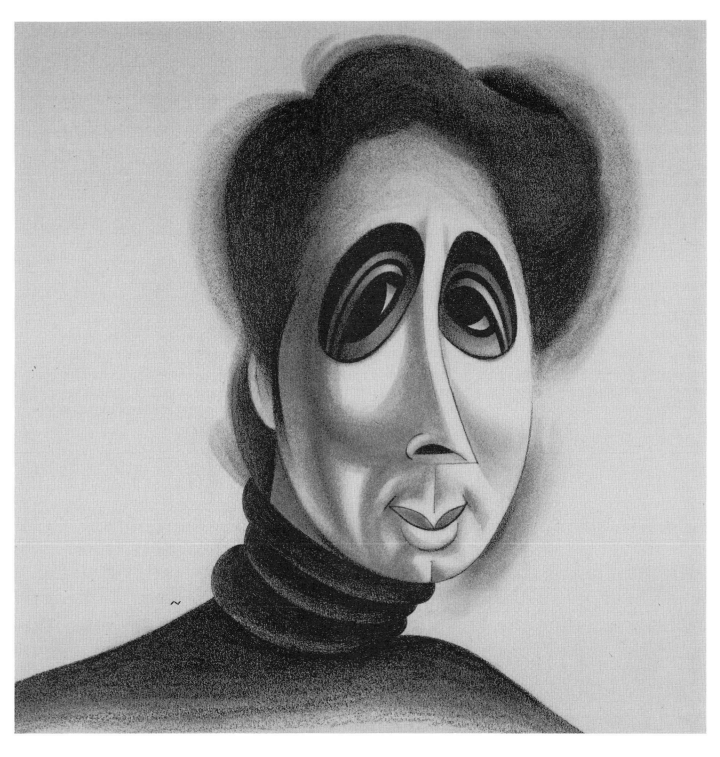

Composer John Corigliano, whose Symphony No. 1 (dedicated to the victims of the AIDS epidemic) was given
its New York premiere by the Philharmonic. 1992.

It was obvious to me and countless others that its original stage design was a mistake. The entire organ mechanism lined the rear stage wall, absorbing rather than reflecting sound. The highly touted organ was cleverly concealed by a mesh scrim, but for recitals it was warmly illuminated and highly visible. As such it was depicted in color on Virgil Fox's LP album recital. Beautiful and mighty as the organ was, the Philharmonic decided to sell the specially constructed instrument. They had no offers and couldn't give it away until a California college, with the help of a donor, moved it to that coast. Today the Philharmonic wheels on stage a puny electronic console when it programs Saint-Saëns's ex-

pansive Organ Symphony. But its new music director, Kurt Masur, fresh from the Leipzig Gewandhaus, finds it culturally provincial for a major symphonic organization to concertize minus a mighty organ, and he vows to install one again. Where will he place it?

Members of the orchestra complained they couldn't hear themselves, so the stage was redone, plaster changed to wood. Hexagonal panels were originally suspended several feet from the ceiling and tilted various ways to "tune" the hall. These were promptly dubbed "coffin lids" because of their shape. Uninformed as to proper behavior, the sound waves dodged between the tuning panels and hit the ceiling just beyond, to be trapped there rather than reflected. The tuning panels were removed.

First the concave walls were straightened. They had been concentrating the sound rather than spreading it. The intimacy induced by the midnight-blue walls was changed to beige to open the sound psychologically. As an artist I found that revelation intriguing. The walls and ceilings became a series of steps, with recessed crystal bowls of light (specially manufactured in a small town in [then] Czechoslovakia on the recommendation of guest conductor George Szell) glowing from the ceiling.

It didn't work. Not for critic Har-

old Schonberg of the *New York Times* anyway. In came Avery Fisher to pay for what is the current hall. The box offices were placed in the entrance lobby where they should have been in the first place, instead of being tucked in the rear. After the interior was gutted, it was completely rebuilt and reshaped. Today its surfaces consist of random staggered angles and corners to spread sound. Horizontal cigarlike cylinders define the boxes and balconies to further disperse the sound. Though the hall has become known for its live acoustics, improvements still abound. Current conductor Masur recently arranged for a series of baffles to be installed on stage.

The New York State Theater, which faces Avery Fisher Hall, opened to house plays, musicals, the New York City Opera, and the New York City Ballet. Composer Richard Rodgers headed The Music Theater of Lincoln Center as a labor of love. Right off, the theater ran into serious problems when Peter Brook brought in his production of *King Lear* with Paul Scofield. No matter how well they enunciated and projected, the cast could not be heard. Brooks cursed the acoustics and panic set in. Improvements were quickly attempted, but it was the first and last time a play was staged there. For several summer seasons Rodgers successfully revived musicals until his overexposed *Oklahoma!* lost money. The Music Theater of Lincoln Center was precipitously ditched in 1969.

King Lear. Paul Scofield commands daughter Cordelia, "Hence, and avoid my sight!" *New York Daily News* 1964.

When popular soprano Beverly Sills took over as director of the New York City Opera, she decided to present musicals as part of the repertory. This stirred dissent among some supporters, but the affluent Lawrence Wien donated five million dollars for the series. Some rarities were revived, like *Brigadoon* and *The Pajama Game*, but with the money exhausted and Sills retired, the project was discontinued. There now remain in the repertory such musicals as *Candide*, *Sweeney Todd*, *Brigadoon*, *Street Scene*, *A Little Night Music*, *The Most Happy Fella*, and *110 in the Shade*, but the company clearly defines them as "operas," not "musicals." Can it be that such maneuvers of nomenclature make funding easier? And if so, who is to champion revivals of the less lofty but equally lovable musicals?

Returning to the acoustical problem; a huge curved sound reflector was eventually installed at the top of the proscenium arch. This feature became part of the New York City Opera logo.

The house has functioned well as a music theater. From the beginning, it was known for the "headlights" which are studded throughout the auditorium for illumination. The theater also boasts a grand promenade with a ceiling as high as the building, completely surrounded by walkways from all seating levels. This is truly elegant, but at the same time, it reminds one of the cell block scenes in the old Warner Brothers prison films.

Below, flanking both ends of the promenade are gigantic marble statues by Elie Nadelman, each one depicting two portly ladies. Television host Alexander King guffawed as he pointed out that they were blowups from miniatures originally the size of an ashtray!

Gun-shy, Lincoln Center officials installed some additional sculpture shaped to fit the lobby's stairwells. These were abstract in style and of "temporary" materials, they said, to test patron reaction. Nobody protested so they remain. The "temporary" materials seem to have held up just fine for over twenty years!

When the fountain in the plaza was completed, I read an announcement that the waters were designed to be "played" by artists from a keyboard somewhere in the State Theater. Its complex of pipes could produce an endless variety of spurts, streams, and colors. Some name artists were scheduled to design and program the waters. By the time I applied, I was quietly informed that the idea had to be abandoned because when "played," the pipes became so overheated that they threatened to self-destruct in a meltdown! No press release on that one. Ever since then, the fountain has maintained a simple sugarloaf shape, or spouts about a foot high in a modest circle around its border. As John Chapman observed it in this phase from the State Theater veranda during intermission, he called it the world's largest bidet. "Yes," I agreed, "but where shall we find a bottom large enough to enjoy its benefits?"

Turning to the Vivian Beaumont Theater building, at the northwest corner of Lincoln Center, we have before it a grand reflecting pool, one foot deep. From the first, it leaked into the cafeteria beneath it. Several years were required to trace and plug the leak. Meanwhile, Henry Moore's large sculpture *Woman* was placed in the pond. Specially designed to be reflected, the piece immediately became a source of controversy. Every work of this British master that I've seen is the epitome of grace, but *Woman* is pinheaded, klutzy, ungainly, and is placed squatting awkwardly in the water. Media protests were so intense, especially from women, that the title was changed to *Figure*. NBC-TV reporter Gabe Pressman revealed that the late Susan Bloch, PR lady at the Vivian Beaumont, quietly engineered the opposition.

Meanwhile, the cafeteria below, planned in part to accommodate backstage performers in costume or leotards, never did catch on. It was geographically inconvenient for them but most convenient for hordes of high school students. These came via the underpass, enroute to their school, just to the rear of Lincoln Center, from their subway station on Broadway, especially in inclement weather. The cafeteria's vinyl upholstery was slashed and security became a problem. The cafeteria was eventually eliminated in favor of administrative offices.

The Henry Moore sculpture in the reflecting pool.

Now for a startling story about the Beaumont. In mid-August 1971, while most theater people were vacationing, a deal was finalized between Lincoln Center and City Center for the latter to take over The Repertory Company of Lincoln Center and its two theaters, the Vivian Beaumont and the Forum (now the Newhouse). The New York City Council voted an appropriation of five million dollars for major alterations planned by City Center.

Serene siestas under beach umbrellas and in hammocks were explosively interrupted as those theater people read of the *fait accompli* in their newspapers. Soon they took to their wheels, planes, Amtraks, or Hampton Jitneys and headed for New York.

Henry Hewes, president of the Drama Desk, called a special panel meeting at Sardi's in September to discuss Lincoln Center and it proved a rallying point to many interested nonmembers such as producer Dore Schary and actress Edith Meiser.

Norman Singer and Richard Clurman, the directors of City Center, revealed plans to convert the large backstage area of the Beaumont (with room for five repertory stage wagons) into administrative offices for City Center. Next they discussed the plan to make the downstairs Forum a movie theater for showings of the Langlois Cinematique (a French film collection it was offered). This involved removal of the revolving stage mechanism for Beaumont repertory productions.

New entrances for the theaters were to be opened on 65th Street, eliminating "the awkward approaches via the plaza or the tunnel."

Finally, the theater's artistic director, Jules Irving, was to be replaced and its "sorry record" improved.

All this from men with concert music and real estate backgrounds, assisted by an architect with a record for designing shopping malls!

Audience objections were voiced against abandoning a rare repertory facility so soon after its installation. Great indignation was expressed at the thought of a theater (whose intimacy was savored by many) turned into a movie house.

The 65th Street entrance idea turned many heads since so much had been written of the joint architectural concept evolved by Harrison, Abromavitz, Johnson, and Saarinen to have Lincoln Center patrons approach all events from one elegant plaza—with an option for doorstep entry underground.

As for the "sorry record" of the theater company, I rose to point out that from the reviews I had read this was simply not true, and I was appointed on the spot by Henry Hewes to obtain the records. This was rapidly done and notices from eleven publications showed two to one approval of its productions, both at the Beaumont and the Forum.

The Drama Desk meeting created an ad hoc committee headed by Dore Schary to investigate the issue further. Meanwhile, as an old Lincoln Center watcher I was rankled by the fact that Jo Mielziner, eminent theater and scenic designer, responsible for the interior of the Beaumont-Forum (Eero Saarinen created the exterior), had not been consulted about the drastic changes. I called Mielziner and asked why not. "I'm hopping mad about all of this," he said. "I was at a Lincoln Center cocktail party some months ago and not a word was said."

With the approval of my editor, Lee Silver, I offered him space in the *Daily News* to tell his side of the story, which he supplied readily. The *News* felt it important enough to give him the entire Op-Ed page.

That shook things up quite a bit. The *New York Times* called Mielziner and asked why he let the *News* scoop them.

"Norkin called me and you did not," was his reply.

In October the Drama Desk led a large delegation to a standing-room-only meeting of the New York City Council Finance Committee, which was holding public hearings (a mere formality) on the five million dollars granted to the City Center for the takeover.

Clive Barnes, then critic of the *New York Times* protested "the mutilation." Jules Irving rebelled at the injustice to his company's record.

Taking note of the many protests, Councilman Carter Burden criticized Chairman Mario Merola for his tolerance. "The five million dollars has already been voted by the City Council. It can't be overturned."

"Sit down, Carter. The law says the public must be heard from," growled Merola.

The ground swell of resentment continued to grow and at its height, City Center, realizing it had alienated the very theater people it needed for its plans to work, withdrew its offer. The Beaumont was saved.

The last major structure to be completed was the Metropolitan Opera House, "large as a forty-six-story building laid on its side." High on the proscenium arch was an abstract piece of sculpture resembling an open bracelet teethed with spikes. It became known as "the beartrap." Numerous chandeliers, suggestive of enlarged snowflakes, were suspended by cables from the ceilings before performances began, and raised out of sight as the houselights darkened. Sure enough, one evening the man forgot to press the button and half the audience had obstructed views.

After the acoustical nightmares encountered by the Philharmonic and the State Theater, everyone at the Met quaked awaiting the verdict. They were lucky. No problem there. A batch of new productions opened during its first week. Samuel Barber's *Antony and Cleopatra* took the stage opening night and disappointed a gala international audience. Barber left the country and stayed away for five years. Backstage facilities were the latest word in theatrical engineering, with three full stage wagons and elevators. They shot the works in Richard Strauss's *Die Frau Ohne Schatten* that first week, but in *An-tony* on opening night, a gigantic sphinx had to be rotated from within by a perspiring crew of stage-hands, because in a mathematical oversight, a comma had been wrongly placed in the specifications for the stage turntable. Engineers built it to carry only 1,500 pounds instead of the 15,000 required!

Streamers. Foreground, l. to r.: Peter Evans, Dolf Sweet, Kenneth McMillan. Background, L. to r.: Mark Metcalf, Terry Alexander, Dorian Harewood. *New York Daily News* 1976.

Leontyne Price and Justino Diaz in the world premiere of *Antony and Cleopatra*, opening night, new Metropolitan Opera, Lincoln Center. *New York Daily News* 1966.

Leonard Bernstein's *Mass*. Alan Titus as the Celebrant. Metropolitan Opera House. *New York Daily News* 1972.

Earlier in this volume I referred to the splitting of the heavens by Boris Aronson in his effects for *The Creation of the World and Other Business*. There is another storm that occurs early in *King Lear* and sets the stage for some of the worst acts of violence and chicanery to be found in Shakespeare. It is usually staged with well-timed thunderbolts, wind machines, and blinding flashes of lightning as the windlashed old monarch commands the skies to unleash all their devastation. Nothing in this storm can match the damage his daughters have visited upon him! And all the while his loyal Fool clings to him, begging him to seek shelter.

Sketching this scene, as typical *King Lear* as any, avoids having to cope with the large cast in the opening scene as shown here in the Louis Calhern version of 1949.

In a unique piece of staging, Lee J. Cobb's *King Lear* at Lincoln Center symbolized Lear's divided lands with three separate crowns, one for each grant to his daughters. When infuriated by Cordelia's coolness, he cleaved her crown with a sword and awarded the halves to her sisters.

King Lear. Stratford, CT.
Morris Carnovsky, Lester Rawlins.
New York Daily News 1963.

King Lear. L. to r.: Barbara Tweed, Patricia Elliott, Marilyn Lightstone, Lee J. Cobb.
New York Daily News 1968.

King Lear. James Earl Jones, Tom Aldredge. *New York Daily News* 1973.

King Lear. L. to r.: Edith Atwater, Jo Van Fleet, Louis Calhern (Lear), Norman Lloyd (Fool), Martin Gabel, Nina Foch. *New York Compass* 1950.

In December 1993, New York classical music radio station WNCN went rock, upsetting many listeners who had depended on it for years. The *New York Times* music critic blamed its owners for lax promotion.

The New York Philharmonic, for decades a national institution offering its live broadcasts, has not been on the air for years—not even on National Public Radio. Swinging into 1994, Broadway listed a total of three straight plays, way down from one hundred eighty-eight openings in 1927 and thirty-six in 1980, according to the *Times*. (Plays are now seen mainly Off-Broadway.)

Years ago, chorus master David Randolph, known for his annual concerts of Handel's *Messiah*, used to conduct a radio program of recorded classical music during which he would regularly ask for audience reaction via the mail. On one occasion he made a point which had a lasting influence on me: CBS used to present a string quartet and was uncertain as to the size or interest of its audience. It requested letters that would determine the quartet's future. Only five people wrote and CBS canceled the program. Randolph said, "You *know* that small response

was no true indication of audience size. It did show that highbrows somehow think it's gauche to write fan mail." So soap opera filled the airtime vacated by the CBS string quartet. Moral: music lovers must make their preferences known.

From my cheap seat in the Carnegie Hall balcony in the early forties I heard a guest conductor of the New York Philharmonic, Dimitri Mitropoulos, a maestro from Greece, lead the string section in his arrangement of Beethoven's String Quartet Opus 131, called by some the master's finest work. The purpose of such an arrangement is to bring to the orchestral listener a great piece to which he might ordinarily not be exposed. And if purists could shelve their prejudices momentarily, they would hear a masterpiece played with greater sweep and dimension. For me it was an unforgettable experience. I watched closely for future Mitropoulos programs. His repertory was rich in scope and included rare (at the time) performances of Mahler. In answer to my letter of thanks for the latter, he confided that the difficulty with performing Mahler was that the lengthy symphonies often precluded other works on the program to placate the unsympathetic. The press was largely hostile to Mahler at the time.

It takes great courage to challenge a negative press, but in one memorable instance in 1947, he played the rarely performed *Alpine Symphony* by Richard Strauss, a then-unrecorded work that I had never heard. Mitropoulos, a mountain climber, performed it with ardor. It is music which conveys all the majesty, mystery, and thrills to be felt on the mountain trails. But for some reason, probably because of its program and the use of a wind machine and thunder sheet, the critics turned vicious whenever it was given. This occasion was no different and although I felt privileged to hear it, I was stunned at the uniform ripping the piece received in the papers the next day.

I have seen critics routinely ask their libraries for packets containing reviews by predecessors, especially when preparing to cover an unfamiliar work. It's as though they fear that thinking for themselves may possibly fly in the face of traditional opinion.

I could barely wait to express my indignation at the insensitive recepmtion. It was necessary to write the maestro immediately to register the appreciation of at least one listener. His answer:

November 25, 1947

Dear Mr. Norkin:

I can't tell you how much I appreciate your letter, especially since I was in a terrible doubt that my effort, as you say, to present this rarely heard work was worthwhile. Lots of fussy people and critics thought it was a waste of time. Very few people noticed at least the way it was played. They all spoke only about bad music and programmatic music and all this stuff.

I must confess that if I use my critical mind I will have to say the same thing, but for God's sake, why cannot listeners do the same thing I do? I also like good serious music, but I don't reject that symphony because it is descriptive or because it has some cheap moments. I think that the work is well written, sincerely written, and it is also connected with other things which are very close to my heart—the description of life in the mountains, and I try to enjoy with my musicians and my audience by exchanging my feelings through the feelings of a composer who, after all, has been in the programs for generations.

Anyway, I am deeply thankful to you for your letter because at least somebody is grateful for hearing that symphony. No one even mentioned the wonderful way the boys played or the love with which I conducted that piece. All my colleagues in the orchestra enjoyed with me playing that music. We tried to overlook some weak moments. Why can't people pass over and look for the good things that are in things and people. Believe me, there were a lot of good moments, but I guess just like in life, there are people always looking for trouble.

Thank you again.

Very gratefully yours,
D. Mitropoulos

Today the *Alpine Symphony* is heard frequently. The advent of the inexpensive LP record made it accessible to all and created a large following for the work, with numerous recordings.

In another letter in 1952, after his appointment as music director, I urged Mitropoulos to stimulate more variety in the concerto repertory by the guest soloists. Every year the concerti were about the same, with the soloists switching their choices. I made specific suggestions, naming many neglected great works, fully aware that he probably felt the same way, but needed this kind of ammunition in his program planning with the Philharmonic board.

It worked! Advance scheduling took two years, but every piece I suggested was performed by Heifetz, Menuhin, Francescatti, Rubinstein, Arrau, Serkin, et al. Mitropoulos sent me his photo signed: "To Sam Norkin—Very Gratefully."

I sketched him several times in the course of my assignments. I also painted him on the Carnegie Hall podium. His untimely death occurred characteristically, while rehearsing Mahler's Third Symphony at La Scala in Milan in 1960.

Dimitri Mitropoulos.
The Saturday Review 1952.

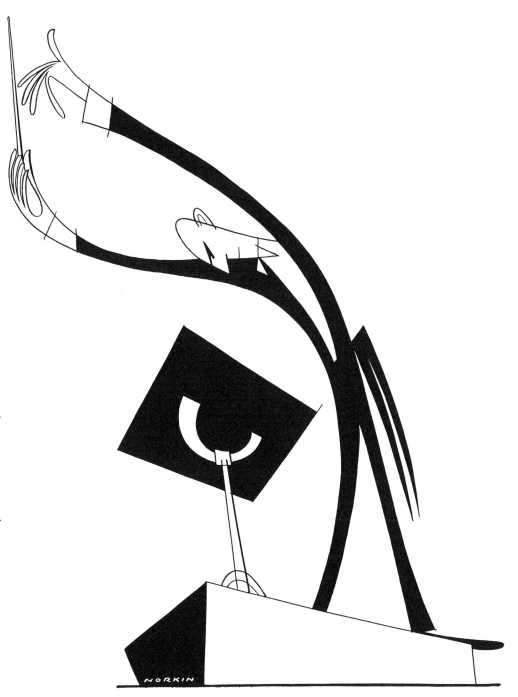

JOSEPH E. LEVINE

In 1954, at the age of fifty-eight, Joseph E. Levine, a late starter as a film producer and distributor, acquired two big money makers with his profits from the Japanese monster movie *Godzilla*. The two new ones were *Atilla*, starring Anthony Quinn and Sophia Loren, and *Hercules*, with beefcake star Steve Reeves. Reeves had a high-pitched voice, so a rich baritone was dubbed in. The film also featured the gigantic ex-heavyweight champ Primo Carnera. For me these were the first of a long series of drawings, which followed, among other things, the blossoming of Sophia Loren into an international star.

Levine also came up with a good share of clinkers. A notable case was a Jules Verne film consisting entirely of animated etching-style drawings. Patrons expecting a film with real actors were disappointed, and one irate man rammed his fist through the box-office window when he was refused a refund.

A huge financial failure was O'Neill's *Long Day's Journey Into Night,* with Katharine Hepburn, Ralph Richardson, Jason Robards, and Dean Stockwell. Ironically, today this flop has artistic stature. Mentioned elsewhere in this volume is *The Threepenny Opera*, with Curt Jurgens and Sammy Davis, Jr., which was withdrawn before distribution.

The same was true for a circus film starring popular Pat Boone; according to Levine, DeMille's *The Greatest Show on Earth* failed to draw, leading him to conclude that there was no audience for sawdust film sagas. (I've always found it curious that producers attribute success or failure to subject matter rather than the treatment of it.)

Levine became the last of the movie moguls, believing in big promotion while armed with the talents of Fellini, de Sica, Mastroianni, Mel Brooks, Zero Mostel, Dustin Hoffman, Katharine Hepburn, Peter O'Toole, and others. Some of my nationally distributed drawings of his films are seen here.

Joseph E. Levine films. Left: Anthony Quinn, *Attila, the Hun.* Right: Steve Reeves, *Hercules Unchained.*

Sophia Loren in *The Raffle* from *Boccaccio '70.* 1963.

Long Day's Journey Into Night (film). L. to r.: Katharine Hepburn, Jason Robards, Dean Stockwell, Ralph Richardson.

The Fabulous World of Jules Verne. 1961.

Donald O'Connor in *Aladdin*, with Vittorio Di Sica as the Genii.

I have a story or two involving *Varsity*, a magazine that flourished decades ago and disappeared along with so many others. Cabaret performers like to underscore their bad luck by boasting how many bistros they've "closed." During the period when the Borscht Circuit suffered an epidemic of failures, one comic proclaimed, "Things are so bad I can't even play 'The Red Apple!'" (A bus stop on Route 17, halfway to the Catskills).

In my own experience I've had the rug pulled out from under on numerous occasions. The *New York Herald Tribune*, my prestigious outlet for twelve years, had bravely emblazoned on their walls the slogan "Beat the *Times*," which in hindsight stirs feelings of sad futility. They exited quietly many years ago.

I was then recommended to the New York *Daily News* by Dick Maney, eminent press agent, and John Chapman hired me promptly, to sketch the theater openings every week for twenty-six years. I had qualms over the then-lowbrow reputation of the *News*, but this was tempered by the exposure to five and a half million readers every Sunday. Chapman used to point out that he had as many highbrow readers in those numbers as did Brooks Atkinson, critic of the *Times*. Apparently they gradually found it easier to get their news from instant television reports, and the circulation dwindled to one-third of its heyday. Bankruptcy and firings have plagued every New York newspaper but the *Times*, which remains the only solvent sheet today. Long Island *Newsday* now prints New York *Newsday* with limited acceptance.

Television's inroads helped do in at least two other of my newspapers, the *Washington Star* and the *Philadelphia Bulletin*, whose famed ad slogan, "In Philadelphia, nearly everyone reads the *Bulletin*" soon turned obsolete. I could see it coming when my drawing of a Philadelphia show, usually splashed across the top of the Sunday Drama Section cover, was switched to page three and replaced on the cover by photos of television shows that were seen in *any* city in the U.S. (You had to *pay* to go to the Shubert Theater but television was *free*.)

I was hired my first day out of the army in 1946 by a prospective new magazine, *USA*, published by Marshall Field. For one year, before publication, I created many full-page illustrations for the "bank," at which point Field was advised by his accountant that he had more to gain by making *USA* a tax write-off than by launching it in the face of postwar inflation. *USA* was DOA. Most of my illustrations were lost.

Stanislawski and his influence on the American Theater. *Theater Review* cover 1978.

I began contributing to a liberal newspaper, *The Compass*, successor to *PM*. It walked a shoestring for three years and folded the night the Eisenhower-Nixon ticket was elected in 1952. *USA*'s editor, Norman Cousins, invited me to contribute to his other publication, *The Saturday Review*. For them I created many cover designs and illustrations until their demise.

I had begun a happy relationship with the renowned *Colliers* magazine just before its collapse.

During the fifties there was a rash venture by a member of the Lipsett family, well known in the salvage field, especially in the case of the fire-ravaged steamer *The Normandie*. You may recall that the French ocean liner was docked in New York when the motherland fell to the Nazis. The United States was converting it to a troopship when an acetylene torch started the fire. When last seen, the sleek *Normandie*, renamed with gigantic letters on its sides, *LIPSETT*, was towed for junk to Jersey City.

Mr. Lipsett loved a good show, so he attempted to float a magazine named *Theater* in the face of past failures in that category. I contributed several articles and illustrations, until it, too, was junked after a few issues.

Another, better attempt was made in the seventies by *Theater Review*. After a few years of using my covers and illustrations, it fell victim to underfinancing.

The only time I ever invested in a show was when producer Alex Cohen persuaded me to plow back my fee for promotional artwork into *The First Gentleman*. It folded fast.

In another case my royalties ceased forthwith for my show curtain of cast caricatures. The presentation was *A Musical Jubilee*, by The Theater Guild. It limped along to its sad end in a matter of weeks.

My sculpture for the musical *Can-Can*, designed in collaboration with Abe Burrows, received the required laughs and appreciation from the critics. The show was a hit and had a good run, perhaps because I received no program credit. As a contributor, I was not a member of the scenic designers' union.

My caricatures adorned the walls of the parking garage at Atlantic City's casino hotel The Atlantis, to perk things up for impatient gamblers. With unseemly haste, the hotel became the first of the new casinos to go Chapter 11.

Nanette Fabray personally defends America in *Arms and the Girl. New York Herald Tribune* 1950.

My appearance as a lecturer-demonstrator on theatrical caricature was the last entertainment at Plum Point, an elegant resort on the banks of the Hudson, before it was shuttered. Later, I blessed the Lake Minnewaska Hotel, a venerable institution in the Shawangunk Mountains, with my special program, which proved to be one of the last things seen there before foreclosure. I appeared regularly over the years at Chesters', an adult resort in the Catskills, known as "An island of culture in a sea of borscht" until it was sold to a girl's camp.

A major triumph took place on the S.S. *Rotterdam* Theater Guild Cruise, where my performance debut held the attention of a sprawling audience in the grand lounge, crossroads of the ship, flanked by busy bars. From his bar stool, the Holland-America VP (let us call him Mr. Lindstrom), was impressed with what he saw, and over drinks, assured me that I would be welcome on all future cruises. I did join the Music, Jazz, and other sails until the line switched to a booking agent with its own entertainers. So I called the Holland-America offices and said I was trying to reach Mr. Lindstrom. "We are too. If you know his whereabouts, let us know. The police are interested as well." It seems there was a financial scandal involving unauthorized investments in a Swiss hotel, made by Mr. Lindstrom. End of the S.S. *Rotterdam* for me.

My many show posters and ads were commissioned through the leading theatrical advertising agency, Blaine-Thompson, which fell victim to deadbeats and went under years ago, dispersing a crackerjack staff.

For a couple of years I supplied a feature for *Playfare*, the off-Broadway program magazine. I was free to sketch and praise off-Broadway highlights. *Playfare* was acquired by *Playbill*, which had their own staffers.

My monthly art reviews for the Carnegie Hall House Program ran for two seasons until *Stagebill* absorbed it and filled it with their own features.

Then there was the recording industry, which proliferated from RCA Victor, Columbia, and Decca into a slew of independents with the development of the LP record. In addition to the big three, I contributed many cover designs to the new smaller labels, such as Westminster, Urania, and Coliseum, but in a few years they too were gone. Some may see in this relentless saga a semblance of versatility. Others may react in the manner of the old MC quip: "Can't hold a job!"

I don't feel too badly about all this. Obsolescence or evanescence seems to be part of the American scheme of things. There's a new Madison Square Garden every few decades. A Coliseum is replaced by a Javits Center in the same time span. Financial wizards work their wonders and vast structures rise or fall.

Returning to *Varsity*. I was asked to create a feature called "My Funniest Experience." I interviewed and sketched celebrities as they told their stories. I found myself in Philadelphia to supply a drawing for the *Herald Tribune* of *Make A Wish*, a new musical starring Nanette Fabray, so I asked her to be my first subject.

She told me that her funniest experience had just happened the other day but it wasn't usable: the venetian blind next to her bed at the Bellevue-Stratford was stuck in the open position, robbing her of privacy. The hotel handyman rang her doorbell at 8 A.M. After a night of rehearsal changes, she had fallen asleep

at 5 A.M. Blearily she staggered to the door, in only her pajama tops, to let him in, explaining to the puzzled mechanic that the faulty blind was subjecting her and her husband to exposure. He promised to return later for the repair. It was only then that she realized her state of undress and the handyman's reaction.

Make a Wish. L. to r.: Herman Melville, Nanette Fabray, Stephen Douglass. *New York Compass* 1951.

The usable story she gave me had to do with a photo contest she entered as a teenager. She ran onto the field at a rodeo to get a shot of a bucking bronco with her Kodak. A security man swept her off her feet as she snapped the photo a split second from flying hooves. Her somersault shot won first prize!

Another story came from Brooklyn Dodger shortstop Pee Wee Reese, known as "The Kentucky Colonel."

"I was on first base while Dixie Walker was at bat. He missed a pitch with a vicious swing and his bat went flying, landing at my feet. Southern gentleman that I am, I walked his bat home and gave it to Dixie. On my return to first base, I was unceremoniously tagged out. Back in the dugout, manager Leo Durocher showed little appreciation for my good manners."

Another baseball incident, now celebrated, came from Casey Stengel, when he was managing the then–second division Brooklyn Dodgers in a game in Philadelphia's Baker Field, known as "the bandbox" because of its short fences, particularly in the right field. Boom Boom Beck, so named in recognition of the hits he

generously surrendered, was on the mound for the Dodgers. This occasion was no different. Casey went to the mound to yank him but Beck refused to leave. Casey insisted, so Beck wheeled and flung the ball as hard as he could, trying to get it over the right-field fence. Hack Wilson, the Dodger right fielder, was daydreaming during the time-out, and when the ball struck the tin fence with a bang, Wilson thought that play had resumed, fielded the ball, and tried to nail the invisible runner at second base while the small crowd had a big laugh.

Casey Stengel.

When a name conductor appears at the Met, I like a rehearsal seat along the curve of the orchestra pit and to the side, from which point I can sketch the maestro in action and also see the stage.

During the preparation of *Falstaff*, Leonard Bernstein found a rough spot in the score. It comes just after Mr. Ford, believing his wife to be unfaithful, delivers his aria despairing of women, to the thunder of trombones.

Ford exits and down the stairs comes Falstaff in his best finery, waltzing off for his date with Mrs. Ford. The blasting trombones descend and bottom out to a whisper as the perfumed strings accompany Falstaff out the door.

"What's wrong?" called Bernstein to the trombone choir. "That's not a hard note to hit down there, in unison!" After a while they got it right. But from where I sat I could spot the problem: the four trombone music stands bore the *Racing Form*, the *Daily News* sports page, *Reader's Digest*, and the *National Enquirer*.

Leonard Bernstein rehearsing Verdi's *Falstaff* at the Met. 1964.

IL TROVATORE

The late Leonard Warren was that rarity in opera, a box-office baritone. Good tenors are scarce, so popularity is understandable. However, there are many fine baritones.

Warren wore his importance with style, often throwing his weight around, which was considerable, and frequently becoming a center of controversy.

One such incident happened at the dress rehearsal of a new production of *Il Trovatore* at the Met. In a third-act duet, dressed in black, wearing menacing makeup as the villainous Count Di Luna, including a Fu Manchu moustache, he was forcing himself on the heroine, Antoinetta Stella. Venerable conductor Fausto Cleva began tapping his baton sharply on his music stand. Warren stopped singing. "I'm sorry, Maestro, we can't sing it that fast. What'll we do when it accelerates later?" Cleva answered, "I'm not asking you to sing fast. Just to keep the time!"

"Well, I don't like the time, Maestro!" and with a final glower, he left the stage.

"Okay, take five," announced a breathless stage manager. From the rear of the cavernous old Met, impresario Rudolph Bing came running down the aisle to placate his leading conductor of Italian repertoire.

Now, I was seated almost behind Cleva, in the second row, hemmed in by my overcoat on one side and my folio on the other. Cleva opened the gate behind him and conferred with Bing right above my head:

"I don't know what's wrong with that man!" said Cleva. "He tell everybody what to do! He tell the designer how to make the scenery. He tell the costumer how to make the costume. He tell the director how to direct, and now he tell ME how to conduct. Why can't he just keep his big mouth shut, and sing!"

From the sketchbook. Leonard Warren as Count di Luna in *Il Trovatore.*

A NEW
FAUST
AT THE MET

One of my many covers for *The Saturday Review* featured a caricature of an important new bass-baritone making his American debut as Mephistopheles, Nicola Ross-Lemeni.

There was one problem. Magazines require several weeks of lead time. That gave me the first day of rehearsal to sketch Mr. Ross-Lemeni without makeup, costumes, or scenery. The latter two items could be perceived from the designs. As to the devil's makeup, Rolf Gerard, the artist who created it, made a drawing for me. In this nineteenth-century concept, Mephisto would have no tail or horns. Instead his hair would simulate horns, his nose would have a hook, and there would be the inevitable Vandyke and moustache.

The drawing seen here shows how I put it all together on time. An early copy of *The Saturday Review* was shown to Ross-Lemeni, and, because he still hadn't had his makeup on, he was horrified at my concept of him, called the magazine, and insisted the issue be withdrawn or he'd sue. Indeed, editor Norman Cousins tried to recall the magazines, but to no avail. The distributor had done his job only too well. It was now available in fifty states.

Meanwhile, Ross-Lemeni took his copy home to his wife. "I have never been so insulted. I will sue!"

"Let me look at it," she said. "Why, Nicky, you are never looking so handsome in your whole life!"

And with that and a couple of phone calls, *The Saturday Review* was off the hook.

NORKIN

Faust.
Nicola Ross-Lemeni as Mephistopheles.
The Saturday Review 1953.

Herbert von Karajan

At age eighty-one, Maestro Herbert von Karajan was unquestionably the world's leading conductor in his age group and, ailing as he was, he limped into New York with the unsurpassed Vienna Philharmonic for three sold-out concerts in February 1989. I made sure to be there because, as one critic put it, at his age and infirmity this could be his valedictory appearance here.

Walking haltingly onstage with the help of one of his musicians and holding onto the shoulder of each fiddler he passed, he made his way to the podium, climbed up, and leaned back against a padded support rail. His fluid arms then gave the downbeat and the program was under way.

Some events trigger flashbacks and this was one of them. In 1967 I arrived at the press office of the Metropolitan Opera to sketch a rehearsal at which von Karajan was conducting and directing the action of Wagner's *Das Rheingold*. As Anne Gordon, press agent of the Met, escorted me down the elevator to the stage, she said I was in for a rare treat and she was correct. This director was not content to tell the singers how to act; he demonstrated. Mime was called upon to writhe and grovel on the ground as he was beaten by the invisible Alberich, and here was our world famous maestro down there with him rolling and kicking, to show just how he wanted it done. Then he would spring up and fly back to his orchestra to resume where he left off with the music.

My flashback ended as the capacity audience in Carnegie Hall gave the fragile maestro an emotional ovation. After several bows, he and the orchestra vacated the stage. The applause and shouts continued. He was led out from the wings again a few paces and waved goodbye for the last time.

Die Walkure. Herbert von Karajan directs, Thomas Stewart (Wotan), and Birgit Nilsson (Brünhilde).
New York Daily News 1967.

LEOPOLD STOKOWSKI

The rehearsal, of course, brings me into contact with great performers in the act of preparation. Some of them can be special and personal. When Leopold Stokowski made his Metropolitan Opera debut, conducting a new production of Puccini's *Turandot*, it was my privilege to sketch him close up at rehearsal.

The legendary maestro, byword of my music-loving youth, did not disappoint. During a break, he consented to pose for my photos. The shots included a pair of crutches resting on the first row behind him, used as the result of a hip injury.

It was some years later, in Abram Chasins's biography of him that I learned he had sustained that injury playing football with his two sons by Gloria Vanderbilt in the hallway of his Fifth Avenue apartment.

Some earlier sidelights: in the thirties Stokowski made his film debut in one of the *Big Broadcast* movies. His actual appearance was preceded by a view of his hands, sans baton, introducing the opening measures of Bach's *Little Fugue* in G Minor. After an extended sequence of manual narcissism the camera oozed back to reveal the rest of Stoky as he guided the fugue to its expansive conclusion. This performance led Oscar Levant, pianist and movie and radio personality, to remark, "I wish I were around when Stokowski discovered his hands."

Another cherished story, entirely unverified, involves his marriage to Gloria Vanderbilt, she in her twenties while he was in his sixties. Vanderbilt, an accomplished artist and designer, was a drama student at the time and was to be picked up at Stokowski's town house by a classmate one evening. When the classmate appeared at the front door, Maestro Stokowski, in house robe and rumpled white mane, was summoned by the maid. From the duplex balcony Stoky informed the youngster below that Gloria had to leave earlier than expected and

would meet her at the studio. Later, Gloria apologized for the mix-up, but her friend assured her graciously, "Your grandmother explained everything," skipping in one fell swoop an entire generation, gender, and relationship.

In a final footnote, his obituary described his last day. He was about to be driven to a London studio to record Rachmaninoff's lush Second Symphony for the first time. This grand romantic work was ideally suited to his gifts, and his sudden death in his nineties robbed us all of what may have been a treasured swan song.

Leopold Stokowski conducting *Turandot* at the Met. Franco Corelli, Birgit Nilsson, and Alessio De Paolis.
New York Daily News 1961.

MR. OUTSIDE AND MR. INSIDE

As I write, twenty-five years have passed since the American premiere of the performing version of Gustav Mahler's unfinished Tenth Symphony. This may not seem like a world-shaking event if you're losing sleep over whether the Forty-Niners will make it to the Super Bowl or the Mets climb out of the cellar.

But please bear with me. The drawings seen here, of composers Jean Sibelius and Gustav Mahler, were sketched to illustrate an excel-lent comparison of the two musical giants and the vicissitudes of their popularity. As fashions in taste would have it, in 1976, when music critic Bill Zakariasen wrote his piece, Sibe-lius had fallen from being the most popular composer with New York Philharmonic audiences in 1935 to a bypassed name since his death in 1957. In the meantime, one of the most maligned names in music, Mah-ler, had not only become standard symphonic repertory, but acquired the aura of chic. Elsewhere in this volume I have attributed this change primarily to the persuasion of Leonard Bernstein, who, as musical director of the New York Philhar-monic, championed Mahler's entire output.

Beginning during the lean years when every Mahler performance brought forth from the influential *New York Times* critic Olin Downes a gusher of invective that inundated composer, conductor, and "mis-guided" listener alike, a dedicated number of Mahler converts banded together to enjoy and defend their favorite. Ever so slowly, with the passing years, they watched in disbe-lief as the master's music achieved the inevitable acceptance in fulfill-ment of his prophesy, "My time will yet come." By 1965 Downes was gone and with him all opposition to the regular performances of Mahler's lengthy and difficult symphonies. All but one.

continued on page 314

Jean Sibelius. *New York Daily News* 1976.

continued from page 312

There remained a facsimile published copy of the score of his unfinished Tenth Symphony, composed on his deathbed in 1911, containing music of profound interest to those who knew what went before. A British musicologist, Deryck Cooke, came up with a performing version of the symphony by bridging the gaps between the finished sequences. He obtained permission from Alma Mahler, the composer's widow, "for a program about the Tenth Symphony" on the BBC in 1960, celebrating Mahler's one hundredth birthday.

Madame Mahler was horrified when she heard the Tenth Symphony was thus performed in the face of her ban of several decades.

We Mahlerites obtained a tape of the broadcast from England and staged a mass copying session. Each of us brought his portable tape recorder and sat spellbound as the long-forbidden sounds took voice. Now it was time for our leaders, annotator Jack Deither and sound engineer Jerry Bruck, to play the tape for the composer's wife so that the world could be permitted to hear what Mahler had in mind during his last days. In her Upper West Side New York City apartment, the elderly lady was in tears as the glorious sounds recreated by Cooke filled her living room. Permission lovingly granted, Diether and Bruck now approached Eugene Ormandy, conductor of the Philadelphia Orchestra, and in September 1965, I joined the Mahlerites in a caravan to Philadelphia's Academy of Music for the premiere.

At my newspaper, the New York *Daily News*, Douglas Watt, our music critic, once wrote facetiously that he would like to have an evening of Met Opera last acts so that he could catch what he was compelled to miss because of review deadlines. He then surmised he would have to forgo the last of the last acts for the same reason. All kidding aside, I arranged for Watt to listen to the BBC performance tape in my living room so that when he reviewed the Philadelphians the following week, he would be familiar with Mahler's exquisite farewell movement, should he have to leave early.

In Philadelphia, Maestro Ormandy welcomed us in his dressing room after the historic premiere, which ushered in another staple in the Mahler repertory.

Gustav Mahler. *New York Daily News* 1976.

The award-winning film *Amadeus* gave wide audiences a supposed glimpse into the personal life of Wolfgang Amadeus Mozart, perhaps the world's greatest musical genius, who had died prematurely almost two hundred years earlier. The vivid portrait made many wonder what it may have been like actually to come in contact with such an "immortal" talent.

In recent decades this was indeed possible, as in the case of Shostakovich, Prokofiev, Stravinsky, Sibelius, and Rachmaninoff, to name a few.

That they were real people, making news like any other mortals, was evident in many ways. Shostakovich lived in fear of liquidation, when at several points his bold music was officially criticized. His opera *Lady Macbeth of Mzensk*, for example, was attacked by Premier Stalin as "muddle, instead of music." He was compelled to withdraw his daring Fourth Symphony while it was still in rehearsal and began to create more palatable symphonies. Many unfettered works were composed for private, smaller ensembles, just as some Soviet painters created closet canvasses. Sweeping as these issues were, I cannot forget one trivial thing that impressed Shostakovich on a rare visit to New York. It was the billboard sign for Camels, puffing smoke rings in Times Square.

The alternately suave and atavistic Prokofiev had similar problems with Soviet criticism. In his case he traveled widely after the 1917 Russian Revolution, returning to the Soviet Union in 1935 to compose the worldwide favorite *Peter and the Wolf.* He showed how he could turn from sardonic works to assuage his obtuse critics with a meltingly beautiful Seventh Symphony. And I remember a human complaint of his, about why he never made it in the United States after the Revolution: "I came from the Far East and entered via 'the back door,' San Francisco."

How inconsiderate of Stalin to die the same day as Prokofiev and smother his obituary.

Sibelius could compose themes for his Russian-occupied land of such nationalistic fervor that, like Irving Berlin's "Alexander's Ragtime Band," they made Finns "want to go to war." This true original shot his bolt by the middle of the twenties and lived on, a quarter of a century later as a legend, near Helsinki. He was the first "modern" composer of my discovery and I sent him his cherished Havana cigars, a scarcity during Finland's isolation in World War II, when a music-loving philanthropist rallied Sibelians worldwide to the cause. I read about with envy and regretted my inability to participate in an excursion by the Philadelphia Orchestra, led by another Sibelian, Eugene Ormandy, when they played the aged master's music on his front lawn during a European tour. Ormandy, like many others, asked the composer if there was truth to a forthcoming Eighth Symphony and was answered with the same silent, furrowed frown. Rumors held that he had destroyed the manuscript as not being up to his standard.

Mozart. Done in by Salieri. *New York Daily News* 1981.

I did connect with another legend of his time, Igor Stravinsky. It was backstage at the old Met during his supervision of the premiere of his opera, *The Rake's Progress*. While Fritz Reiner conducted and George Balanchine directed, Stravinsky advised, and I made pencil drawings of the composer for the cover of *The Saturday Review*. During a break, I encountered Stravinsky and asked if he would autograph my drawing of him. He answered, "Iss verry nice, bott I nevaire sign." I showed it to Irving Kolodin, my editor at *Saturday Review*, asking for an O.K. to do a stylized tempera version of it, but he insisted on using the authentic pencil version "as is." Years later, editor Mike O'Neill ran the same drawing with Stravinsky's obituary in the *New York Daily News*.

Finally, I was privileged to attend performances by that great "triple threat," the piano virtuoso Sergei Rachmaninoff, better known as a much-loved composer and, early in his career, as a fine conductor. He enjoyed a long relationship with the Philadelphia Orchestra and on the occasion of his sixty-fifth birthday, in 1938, his compositions made up a Rachmaninoff Festival. Ormandy swept into Carnegie Hall with some four concerts that included Rachmaninoff himself as pianist in his four concerti, plus the *Rhapsody on a Theme of Paganini*. He also conducted the final concert that included his rarely heard choral symphony, "The Bells," as well as the Third Symphony.

This historic series was bound to be one of the all-time highlights of my concertgoing and I was well aware of it at the time. At its con-clusion I sat spellbound in my balcony seat, hands numb from applauding for the ages. Eventually, the orchestra left the stage and most of the audience went home. Some diehards remained, reluctant to let the evening end. One zealot, at the very top of the house, repeatedly called out "RACHMANINOFF, RACHMANINOFF!" through cupped hands. Everyone was now gone, but the house lights remained on. Finally, from the wings, Sergei Rachmaninoff appeared with his black, Persian lamb–collared coat over one shoulder, Russian style. He took one slow step onto the stage, waved wearily to the balcony and left.

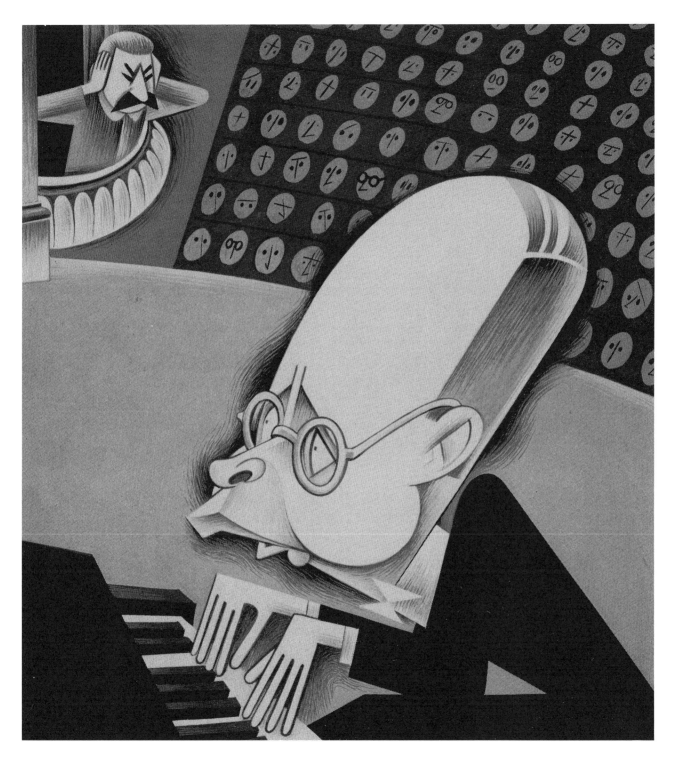

Prokofiev censured by Stalin. *Reporter Magazine* 1949.

Five years later, during the height of the Soviets' struggle against the Nazi onslaught in World War II, Russian aristocrat Rachmaninoff came to the aid of the motherland with a concert in Carnegie Hall for Russian War Relief. This unifying act of nationalism meant more to the morale of the Soviet Union than the several thousand dollars raised, and years later, when I visited the vast Leningrad cemetery containing the countless seige victims in common graves leading to an imposing war memorial, I heard one piece by Rachmaninoff, repeated in various forms via discreet loudspeakers in an otherwise silent park. It was the poignant "Vocalise," a wordless song for soprano, fitting in more ways than one. The mourning was common to all Russians, regardless of class.

Sergei Rachmaninoff. Record album cover.

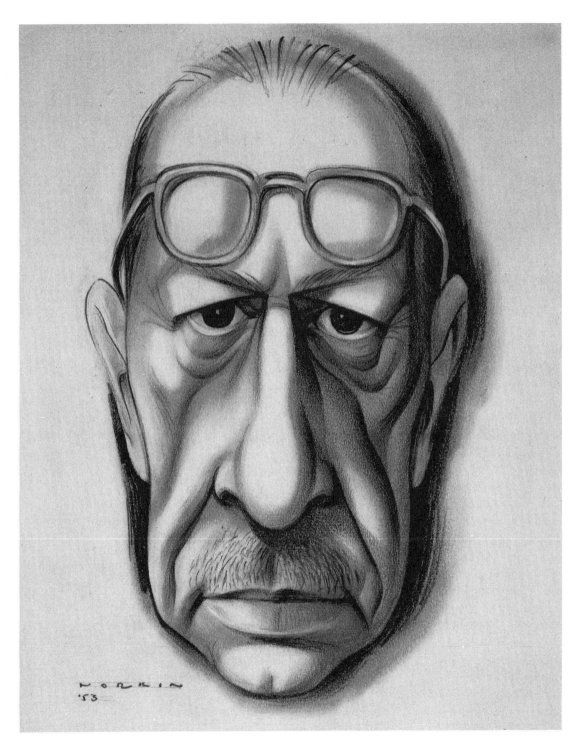

Igor Stravinski. *The Saturday Review* 1953.

Robert Lawrence, newly added to the music and dance reviewing staff of the *Herald Tribune* in 1942, thought it would save space and coverage to illustrate ballet events with montage drawings. Through our many office conversations he knew of my interest in dance. From the first, I had been curious to see the movements that accompanied, for example, Borodin's *Polovetsian Dances*, Debussy's *Afternoon of a Fawn*, and any number of other symphonic works that used to be standard fare on the programs of the Ballet Russe at the old Met. Happily I found my girlfriends equally enthusiastic, despite a location just under the ceiling in the Family Circle. From now on I would be in orchestra seats, where the facial expressions of the dancers were part of the art.

Lawrence assigned me to sketch a new ballet by an American dancer and choreographer, Agnes de Mille. It had a cowboy setting, with music by American composer Aaron Copland. It was called *Rodeo*.

I met with de Mille in the Russian Tea Room. My drawing was to appear the Sunday before the Ballet Russe season opening. The production was in its early stage, but de Mille came prepared. Her folio bulged with costume and scenery sketches and photos of her male lead, Frederic Franklin. Here she was, in person, to describe her bal-

let, to demonstrate, in the aisle, key poses for me to draw.

Rodeo was a smash in every department. As a consequence, Rodgers and Hammerstein engaged de Mille to choreograph the plot-laden dances of *Oklahoma!*, *Carousel*, and *Allegro*. She was to have a lasting influence on dance for the musical stage.

Numerous triumphs continued in musicals as well as for ballet companies and it was always a pleasant reunion with her at a rehearsal, where I had the chance to sketch the real thing, under her guidance, not just from sketches, photos, and descriptions. She told me of her respect for the artistic level of dance in musicals. Much more rehearsal time and better production budgets were available to the choreographer than in classical ballet.

At one of those rehearsals—for *Goldilocks*—I referred to our first meeting sixteen years earlier for the world premiere of *Rodeo*. She then bemoaned the fact that the costumes and sets were destroyed when the Ballet Theatre's property truck burned in southern France en route to the Brussels World's Fair. Thus, the one ballet our State Department most wanted performed at the Fair was replaced by *Swan Lake*.

Unfortunately, a time came when *New York Times* dance critic Clive Barnes downgraded her. Perhaps her

Above: Agnes de Mille.
Below: Rodgers and Hammerstein.

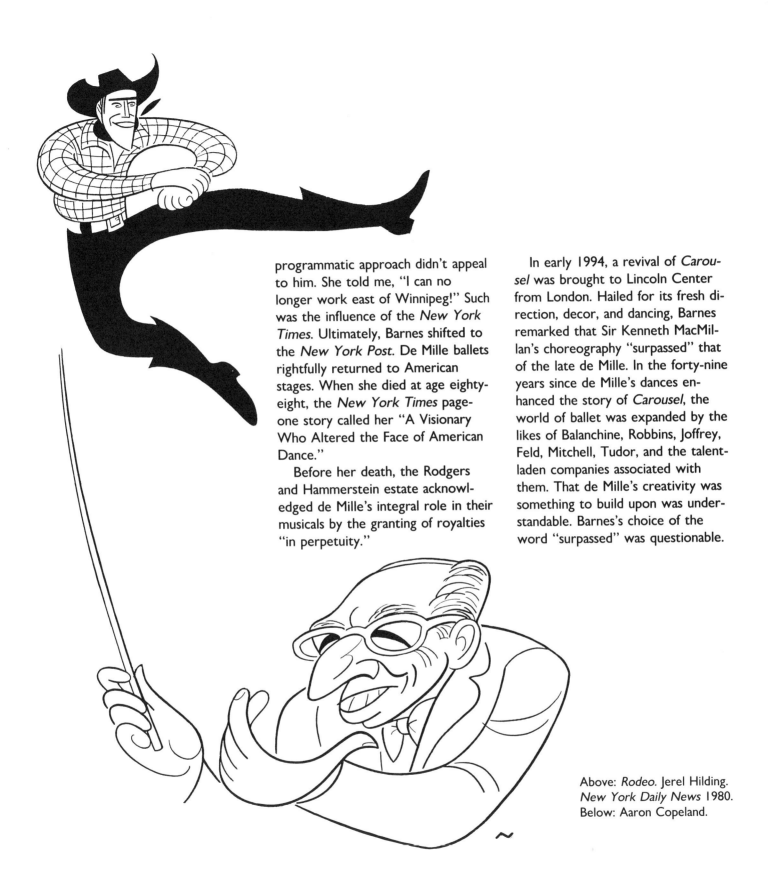

programmatic approach didn't appeal to him. She told me, "I can no longer work east of Winnipeg!" Such was the influence of the *New York Times*. Ultimately, Barnes shifted to the *New York Post*. De Mille ballets rightfully returned to American stages. When she died at age eighty-eight, the *New York Times* page-one story called her "A Visionary Who Altered the Face of American Dance."

Before her death, the Rodgers and Hammerstein estate acknowledged de Mille's integral role in their musicals by the granting of royalties "in perpetuity."

In early 1994, a revival of *Carousel* was brought to Lincoln Center from London. Hailed for its fresh direction, decor, and dancing, Barnes remarked that Sir Kenneth MacMillan's choreography "surpassed" that of the late de Mille. In the forty-nine years since de Mille's dances enhanced the story of *Carousel*, the world of ballet was expanded by the likes of Balanchine, Robbins, Joffrey, Feld, Mitchell, Tudor, and the talent-laden companies associated with them. That de Mille's creativity was something to build upon was understandable. Barnes's choice of the word "surpassed" was questionable.

Above: *Rodeo*. Jerel Hilding. *New York Daily News* 1980. Below: Aaron Copeland.

THE DYBBUK

Because of the trial-and-error nature of rehearsals, most performers would prefer that none but those closest to the production be present. Alas, the public will be asked to attend eventually, so it is necessary to generate excitement and sell tickets early on. Still, some stars don't give a damn and in the case of a mercilessly tight schedule for a new ballet, *The Dybbuk*, choreographer Jerome Robbins and composer-conductor Leonard Bernstein demanded and got total privacy.

Virginia Donaldson, press agent for the New York City Ballet, called me to discuss her dilemma. This was to be the first reunion of the team that created *West Side Story* some sixteen years earlier. Obviously, no photos were possible because the production was still in the process of creation. Could I look at the costume and scenery sketches and talk to the stage manager and come up with some kind of advance drawing?

As she was proposing this difficult formula, another idea came to me. A couple of years earlier, while I was a pinch-hit critic for the *Daily News*, I reviewed the entire New York City Ballet's Stravinsky Festival, a major event including several new and old Robbins ballets. I suggested Virginia show Robbins my seven reviews of the festival. This she did, with the result that Robbins invited me to attend, the only outsider to be there.

In addition to scooping everyone else with my drawing, I was treated to an orchestra rehearsal where Bernstein was putting the finishing touches on the score of an important new work. Ditto for Robbins on the choreography.

Helge Tomassin and Patricia McBride in *The Dybbuk Variations. New York Daily News* 1972.

BALANCHINE AND BALLET

On one occasion I asked George Balanchine, probably the leading choreographer of his time and artistic director of the New York City Ballet, whether he minded the performances of his ballets by other companies—something that was happening with increasing frequency.

Balanchine's answer, in his Russian accent, was as follows: "Let me give an example of how I am feeling about this. I love to play the piano, but I play badly. And as badly as I play, that's how ambitious I am about what I play. So I try to tackle Brahms's Second Piano Concerto, and I really play it badly, but I *love* it! That's why I understand those other companies when they dance my ballets. They do them badly, but they love them. Let them enjoy themselves!"

And while on the subject of the New York City Ballet: From your seat what you see on stage may be poised, ethereal, and glamorous, but on a visit backstage I read the following warning on the company bulletin board:

Dancers may not chew gum on stage.

Park gum in waste baskets, not on walls.

Do not wipe sweaty hands on stage velours.

Dancers may not go into audience while house lights are up.—Wait until house is dark, only after a ballet has begun.

Do not go into audience in costume.

Do not dress in costume until shortly before you are on.

Do not drag costumes on dirty floor.

Seen here are several New York City Ballet drawings and samplings of those sketched for the other fine companies.

George Balanchine. Front page *New York Daily News.* Drawing originally appeared in *The Saturday Review* 1950.

Balanchine's *A Midsummer Night's Dream*, New York City Ballet. Melissa Hayden, Roland Vasquez.
New York Daily News 1962.

New York City Ballet. *Union Jack.* L. to r.: Suzanne Farrell, Peter Martins, Jacques d'Amboise, Patricia McBride, Jean-Pierre Bonnefous. *New York Daily News* 1976.

Parade, currently in the repertory of the Metropolitan Opera. Joffrey Ballet. L. to r.: Acrobats: Dennis Poole, Ingrid Fraley. Chinaman: Gary Chryst. American Girl: Lisa Slagle. 1978.

The Moor's Pavane. National Ballet of Canada. L. to r.: Mary Jago, Rudolf Nureyev, Winthrop Corey.
New York Daily News.

THE NAKED FACE
EXPLORING THE TECHNIQUE OF CARICATURE

From *CARTOONIST PROfiles* magazine:
"Sam Norkin has adapted the following article from his forthcoming book, *Theater Drawings—Theater Stories!* He describes, with remarkable candor, all of the myriad details pertaining to a person to be caricatured. We have never before read such an explicit description of this art."

A few years ago, a group of leading caricaturists were sketching the public at a benefit for indigent cartoonists, sponsored jointly by the National Cartoonists Society and the New York Telephone Company. A *New York Times* reporter interviewed the artists for her column and I found myself wildly misquoted in next day's paper: defining caricature, I called it exaggeration of the *entire likeness* (not just "the most prominent feature"). Instead I was quoted as calling caricature "*an anti-likeness.*" Exactly the opposite of its purpose!

Sometimes statements are not clearly heard, sometimes not understood. So let me set forth my thoughts on what I am convinced is a high art form that is rarely mastered. The term "caricature" has been universally applied as something overdone and inferior; or, a display of poor judgment, of unrestrained behavior or rendition.

These negative literary associations of the term have prevented proper identification of some of the greatest caricaturists. I refer to Modigliani, Picasso, Feininger, van Gogh, and many others who gave invention, design, and fantasy to their portraiture.

If we expressed ourselves in a straight, factual manner we would be rejected as square and dull. Indeed, writers are measured by their use of color and image in their descriptive process. The same standards are applied to portraits. The literal ones are apt to be uninteresting. The better ones are usually more interpretive and, if the likeness is given inflection by the caricaturist, the resulting exaggeration will be most effective of all. It will look just like the subject only more so and the viewer will usually react with amusement or awe at the daring extremes of the artist.

For these reasons I feel the caricaturing art justifies itself per se. Caricature can be applied in countless ways: politics, sports, performing arts, etc. No matter. The principles are the same: to give greater inflection to the personality by taking liberties with proportion. As some express it: "To arrive at the truth by lying."

In writings about art you will encounter much that is pretentious and abstruse. One leading caricaturist tells us his creations are the result of a mysterious process which he himself cannot understand. Others may suspect him of guarding his trade secrets from potential competitors in exactly the same manner as a manufacturer concealing his chemical formulas or a chef his recipes. Personally, I am not concerned about revealing what I've learned over decades of sketching thousands of plays and subjects who have sat for me. I will set it forth freely because a basic ingredient in becoming a true caricaturist is the intensive numerical input that ultimately has you sketching every conceivable subject. New York City offers the artist every social and national type. I don't suppose that Copenhagen has the same fertile ground for the caricaturist.

What then, is the technical process? As mentioned earlier, it is not a matter of exaggerating "the most prominent feature." Most people have no such feature, but everyone is theoretically caricaturable because he has an individual likeness. Therefore I aspire to my definition of the true caricaturist: he can catch everyone—not merely the salient personalities but also the bland, the nondescript, and the dull. True, some are more difficult to capture than others, but all are possible. Remember, too, that a caricaturist sees most people as salient in the first place.

You may have observed that certain features go together. The combinations are infinite and the causes are genetic, racial, or national, lending themselves to fluid linear connection. Ever alert to clues, the caricaturist will find such types helpful. Sometimes I am amused to encounter an offspring of two widely disparate parents, whose physical genes are opposite in every way. A long nose versus a button, bulging eyes against deep slits, hatchet face with jutting jaw opposed to a round head with no chin at all. The result is a draw. Nobody wins, least of all the pitiful subject, sporting a clumsy, illogical face. Nature, however, usually guards against such anomalies by letting one parental set of genes win out over the other.

The caricaturist must determine immediately the likeness factors of his subject. As I view the person before me, I have a vision of the anatomical norm in mind that I automatically equate with him. To the extent he departs from that norm in any detail is what I seize upon to dramatize. The anatomical norm, of course, is learned in any elementary life class or found in a textbook.

There are endless variations of all the factors, from posture and shape of the head to the nature of specific features and their *relationship to each other*.

Laurence Olivier, speaking of makeup, pointed out a mistake in the technician's workup of his face for the role of the Mahdi Sheik in the film *Khartoum*. All features had been equally enlarged, resulting in a huge head. This had to be corrected. In *Richard III*, Olivier was in charge so he emphasized only the nose, creating a unique effect of villainy, which, combined with the hump, was quite sufficient.

But before you touch pencil to paper, conceive your model to best advantage. My art school instructors circled the studio to adjust the pose so each student got a fair shake. A business man I knew had doubts about a painting he had acquired and asked for my opinion. I laughed aloud when I viewed it, because the artist had produced a highly skilled rendering of an awkwardly posed Spanish dancer.

Vivien Leigh and Laurence Olivier in *Caesar and Cleopatra. New York Compass* 1951.

Awkwardness is a concern, but more important is an angle or attitude which reveals the best likeness factors. In the few seconds you have before you start, observe your model talking, smiling, or being serious. Full face, profile, or three-quarters. Observe his natural attitude and what it reveals. Does he tend to look straight ahead, glance downward or upward? What happens to the features, especially the eyes, during these changes? Or to the angle of the head, up, down, or tilted, as it affects the features, their relationship, pattern, or connection?

Here's just an inkling of what you must automatically observe and commit to a premeditated concept in seconds:

If there is one prominent "feature," it has to be the shape of the head. It is elementary to a good likeness. Get it wrong and it will defeat the remaining perceptions. Capture it and you are on your way.

The hair: How much of it? The shape of it. The ratio to the entire head, to the forehead. Above all, the *style* of the hair or hairdo in the case of a woman.

The forehead: the ratio of size and *angle* to the rest of the face. The eyebrows: How thick? How apparent? Do they exist at all? Are they matched or asymmetrical? Where are they located and at which angle? Are they part of the eye structure or way above them? Joined or individual?

The eyes: Set close or wide apart? Large or small? Wide open or shut? Hidden under the brow? Dark lashes or none? Eye liner or eye shadow? Lidded and expressive or squinting in laughter? Bags below or a normal eye muscle? *Light* or *dark*? Angled upward or down? The degree of visible iris, which indicates expression. Are glasses involved? Don't just apply them to the face. They are another factor to incorporate with the eyes. Sometimes they hide the eyes. You must decide how much the glasses condition the look of the subject.

Now the nose: First, the angle, then the shape, the size, the relation to the eyes it separates and the lip it shades. Does it dominate or practically disappear? Wide bridge or narrow? Visible nostrils? Round or elongated? Slanting up or down?

I have been describing the scanning process top to bottom, but starting a portrait with the nose and constructing from that point is a sound approach because of its strategic central placement.

The mouth: Smiling or serious? Fully lipped or just a slit? Close to the nose, hidden by it??! Or far below? Overbite or underbite? Small or large? In an open state, or clamped shut? Wide or pursed? Curved or positioned in expression? Asymmetrical or balanced? Corners up or down? How related to chin, jaw, cheeks, nose? In laughter note the nature of the teeth. How visible? Long? Protruding? Note the gums.

Kevin Kline was seen brooding before his dressing room mirror while rehearsing *Hamlet*. The questioner assumed he was depressed by the problems of the role. "No, I can handle that, but there's nothing I can do about my potato nose and I have no upper lip!"

The chin: strong or receding to the point of nonexistence. Fullness below or squared off. Related to a long neck or no neck at all! Related to full cheeks or a lean face. How does the jaw line travel to the ear? What kind of ear?

Into the neck: How long? What of its angle? Full or thin? How does it and the entire head set into the shoulders; into the collar? Vital body language is involved in the attitude of the neck and shoulders.

Down into the chest and arms, with awareness of line, angle and pose.

Now consider the factor of age. As we grow older we become "more so." Maturity means ripeness. I like Lincoln's quote: "By the time a man is forty, he's responsible for his face." It is indeed difficult to hide the effects of time on the face. I am impressed to note that in some corporate quarters, graphologists pass on applicants for employment on the basis of their handwriting. If these seemingly arbitrary wiggles are a revelation, consider what the naked face tells us, exposing, for all to see, avarice, jealousy, pride, determination, sensuality, fear, indifference, obtuseness, stupidity, disillusionment, despair, defeat, the ravages of time, suffering, and illness—or, serenity, love, honesty, generosity, compassion, wisdom, intelligence, purity, and innocence.

As we go back in time, all the way to infancy, the clues are fewer. A baby may yield the muted, delicate likeness factors that make this one different from other infants. It will also remind you what a luxury it is to sketch *anyone* older than that!

Finally a vital consideration: the technique of the artist itself. Before the Cubists, caricaturists were akin to taffy pullers or clay sculptors, who pulled or pushed a malleable head to distort the features in making their statements. Many pursue this approach today.

The Cubists of 1910–1917 showed an awareness of the design and abstract form to be found in a head or figure. A number of modern caricaturists emerged who have been exploring design inventiveness ever since. I subscribe to this school whenever possible. The exploration of such potential in a face can result in surprising discovery. If subtlety or simplicity suits your subject, the caricature can be particularly satisfying. If the artist is a stylist to begin with, caricature is the perfect medium of expression. There is much talk, for example, about the difference between caricaturing a man or a woman. The modern woman is all style, from her makeup to her hairdo, her clothes, her ornament, she defines her self-image to the artist. On the other hand, the normal male offers no such clues, so you are free to explore an even wider range of interpretation.

Once you have applied those precious few seconds of scrutiny and have established your concept mentally, it is possible to plunge into your drawing, committing your premeditation to paper spontaneously, without roughs, to produce a finished caricature! Try it.

INDEX OF DRAWINGS

ABOUT THE AUTHOR

For more than fifty years, Sam Norkin has been where the theatre is happening, and for more than fifty years, he's captured what he has seen with the keen, clear eye of a discerning caricaturist. In many cases, Norkin's drawings are the only visual record we have of a production!

Norkin's art training began with a scholarship to the Metropolitan Art School (later known as the Rumson Art School) and continued at the Brooklyn Museum Art School and several other institutions.

Norkin's weekly theatre drawings appeared in the *New York Daily News* for twenty-six years. For fifteen years his caricatures were also seen weekly by the readers of the *New York Herald Tribune*. His art has also appeared regularly in the *Washington Post*, the *Washington Star*, the *Philadelphia Inquirer*, the *Philadelphia Bulletin*, the *Boston Globe*, *TheaterWeek*, *Variety*, *Back Stage*, *American Theater*, and *Stages*. Since 1940, Norkin has sketched over 4000 theatrical productions.

Norkin was honored by the League of New York Theaters and Producers (now known as the

League of American Theaters and Producers) with a special award in 1980 "For Outstanding Contributions as a Theatrical Artist." The National Cartoonist Society recognized his theatre illustrations in 1980 with its Special Features award and again in 1984 with its Silver T-Square award "for his exceptional service and devotion to our profession, presented with the esteem and affection of his fellow members."

Norkin has had one-man shows in the Museum of the Performing Arts, Lincoln Center; the Museum of the City of New York; the Metropolitan Opera House, New York; and many galleries.

In *Sam Norkin: Drawings, Stories*, 266 of Norkin's drawings have been brought together for the first time along with his own reminiscences about theatre, opera, ballet, and even the circus.